T.J. COLES studies the philosophy
tion at the University of Plymouth, UK, with reference to
the aesthetic experiences of the blind and visually impaired.
He is director of the Plymouth Institute for Peace Research
(PIPR), author of *Britain's Secret Wars* (2016) and his political writings have appeared in the *New Statesman*, *Lobster*,
Peace Review, *Z Magazine* and axisoflogic.com. He was
shortlisted for the Martha Gellhorn Prize for journalism in
2013.

THE GREAT
BREXIT
SWINDLE

WHY THE MEGA-RICH AND FREE MARKET FANATICS CONSPIRED TO FORCE BRITAIN FROM THE EUROPEAN UNION

T. J. COLES

CLAIRVIEW

Clairview Books Ltd.,
Russet, Sandy Lane,
West Hoathly,
W. Sussex RH19 4QQ

www.clairviewbooks.com

Published in Great Britain in 2016 by Clairview Books

A CIP catalogue record for this book is available from the British Library

Print book ISBN 978 1 905570 81 2
Ebook ISBN 978 1 905570 82 9

Cover by Morgan Creative ('X' graphic © iiierlock xolms; gesturing man
© Blend Images – Masterfile)
Typeset by DP Photosetting, Neath, West Glamorgan
Printed and bound by 4Edge Ltd, Essex

I belong to no island,
With lines drawn across sea shores and thick forests.
Like the tree whose roots recognise no state lines or county
    boundaries,
My feet are the wings that carry this fragile bird over continents.
Go ask the swallow about freedom.
Dare question the great humpback over which swell of ocean it
    belongs to.
These territories dissolve with each creature and every subversive
    border crossing.
Born of the earth we must honour its vast canvas with our
    wandering feet.
Bare skin to soil with no direction,
Just for a while and see where it takes you.
See no sign posts, states or street names,
And be unsure of the known lines you have crossed.
You can be certain of few names here.
This place defined by sense alone.
The ground on which you stand, the state.
Be held by this belonging to a nation, earth,
And move on with this place as your home.

A Nation, Earth by Best Left Wild (Rob Dickinson)

Contents

GLOSSARY & ACRONYMS

AFL-CIO   American Federation of Labor and Congress of Industrial Organizations

AIFMD   Alternative Investment Fund Managers Directive

Brexit   Britain's exit from the European Union

CETA   Comprehensive Economic and Trade Agreement

CIA   Central Intelligence Agency (US)

Customs Union   A trading bloc including common external tariffs

DFID   Department for International Development (UK)

EC   European Commission

ECB   European Central Bank

ESMA   European Securities and Markets Authority

European Free Trade Association   Members include Iceland, Liechtenstein, Norway, and Switzerland

Eurosceptic   A person or group opposed to either the European Union or the Eurozone, or both

EU   European Union

Eurozone   European Union Member States which trade with the euro currency

Free Market   A propaganda term for trade and investment between two or more countries where barriers and restrictions to trade and investment are reduced or eliminated. In reality the stronger of the trading/investing partners often retains hidden tariffs and state-controls, such as subsidizing domestic agriculture

Free Trade (Agreement)/FTA   See above

G7   Group of Seven

G20   Group of Twenty

GDP   Gross Domestic Product

GMO   Genetically-modified organism

IMF   International Monetary Fund

ISDS   Inter-state dispute settlement

ISIL   Islamic State of Iraq and the Levant

ISIS   Islamic State of Iraq and Syria (also ISIL)

Mercosur   A sub-regional bloc consisting of Argentina, Brazil, Paraguay, Uruguay, and Venezuela

Neoliberalism   The deregulation of domestic and, through bi- or multi-lateral agreements, foreign controls on goods and services, especially financial services

MI5   Military Intelligence Section 5 (UK)

MI6   Military Intelligence Section 6 (UK)

MIFID   Markets in Financial Instruments Directive

MoD   Ministry of Defence (UK)

RMB   Renminbi, the currency of China

Single Market   A trading bloc free of restrictions and tariffs

NAFTA   North American Free Trade Agreement

NATO   North Atlantic Treaty Organization

OECD   Organization for Economic Cooperation and Development

TISA   Trade in Services Agreement

Troika   The IMF, ECB and EC

TTIP   Transatlantic Trade and Investment Partnership

UNCTAD   United Nations Conference on Trade and Development

WTO   World Trade Organization

Preface

If you voted to Leave the European Union, the chances are you've been swindled.

It wasn't Brussels that harmed the British public in the wake of the global financial crisis. Brussels mostly hurts those over whom it has power; the Portuguese, the Irish, the Greeks and the Spanish: or PIGS, as the technocrats dismissively call them. Through regulatory opt-outs, Britain ensured that Brussels would have no power over the UK economy. Rather, it was the British government's dedication to an economic policy called neoliberalism (broadly defined below) which has so harmed working people. If anything, the bureaucratic nature of the European Union slowed the workings of neoliberalism. That's why a powerful sector of the UK's policy-making elite want out.[1]

The people advancing the global policy of neoliberalism wanted Brexit. They want more deregulation, more privatization and more internationalism at the expense of domestic investment and production. Most of the working and unemployed persons who voted for Brexit did so for the opposite reason: they want *less* neoliberalism. By funding the Leave campaign, the pro-Brexit elite not only made Brexit happen, they made it look as though they share the interests of ordinary working people on vague notions of sovereignty.[2]

This short book documents some of the wealthy hedge

funds which got even richer betting on the financial volatility caused by the shock outcome of the referendum. It also documents some of the already mega-rich market players who successfully bet on the rise and fall of currencies.

This book is about the Great Brexit Swindle: how, despite the promises of pro-Brexiteers, immigration will continue, as will the privatization of public services, economic globalization via 'free trade', and how the working people of Britain will be put in competition with working people and production from countries with huge populations of poor people, including Brazil, China and Mexico.[3]

Chapter 1 documents who was behind the Leave campaign, how much money they donated, how much money they and their companies have, and how they wanted a Brexit in the years running up to the referendum. Chapter 2 analyses some of the free marketeer internationalists in the British government, many of whom were members of the Leave campaign. Chapter 3 is about Britain and the EU's potential and actual trade and investment deals with Canada and the USA. It compares these countries to Brazil and Mexico, demonstrating how the UK will seek to exploit the latter's cheap labour. Chapter 4 shows that China's economy is dependent on Western investment in its captive labour force and compares it to India's neoliberalism. South Korea's population is wealthier than China's and India's, and suggests that Britain will seek to exploit South Korea's financial services.

The real reasons for Brexit
Mainstream media told us that, out of the goodness of their hearts, Britain's Conservative government allowed the British

public to vote on whether or not to Remain in the European Union. For some unknown reason, the government pledged to hold a referendum on the Europe question no later than the year 2017. Why did they choose to hold it at all? In 1973, the Conservative government of Edward Heath forced Britain into the EU's forerunner, the European Economic Community, without a vote. It was only because Harold Wilson's Labour government held a referendum in 1975 that the public had any say on whether or not to Remain. And why did the Cameron government hold the referendum a year early, in June 2016, at a time of heightened Euroscepticism?[4]

The truth is that Brexit happened for a number of reasons, none of which have anything to do with the wishes of the public. Had the government wished to Remain in the EU, they would have continued their policy of refusal. Successive governments put off holding a vote for over 40 years. The real reasons for Brexit are as follows:

Number one: Britain follows America's lead on most issues and Brexit serves America's financial and geopolitical interests. The right-wing Heritage Foundation describes America's initial interest in a United Europe as a bulwark against the Soviet Union. As the Soviet Union expanded into Eastern Europe, a united West was a good idea. As there is no Soviet Union, there is no need for a United Europe. A regulated European Union, which erects barriers to US products and services (such as labels identifying genetically-modified foods and regulations against privatization) is bad for America's corporate profits. After the Financial Crisis 2008, Europe's central command in Brussels started regulating financial markets in an effort to prevent another crash. The Heritage Foundation report analyses America's efforts to use Britain as a 'Trojan Horse' to push through state deregulation in Europe. As Britain was not powerful enough to do this, America felt that a weakened Europe would better serve its financial and trade interests.[5]

Number two: hedge funds. A small number of very wealthy, London-based hedge fund CEOs decided to get revenge on Brussels, which adopted some regulations in the aftermath of the financial crisis. Hedge funds are financial services institutions which make money betting on the rise and fall of prices, performances, currencies and just about anything you can think of. London is the most deregulated city in Europe. By 2006, it hosted 66% of Europe's 1,400 hedge fund companies. The biggest are based in Mayfair. In the long-run, hedge funds never lose because they hedge their bets on several outcomes and spread their risks. The liquidity firm Citigroup says that by 2018, the hedge fund industry will be worth over $4.8 trillion globally. The biggest CEOs of these companies didn't like Brussels dictating policy and regulation to them and, as we shall see, started backing the Leave camp.[6]

Number three: internationalism. For the last six years, the Tories have been evaluating Britain's role in Europe, commissioning a series of reports from 2012–13, in which the benefits of Remaining in Europe were assessed. On balance, it was decided that Britain should Remain, but should simultaneously distance itself from Brussels; in part by investing much more in the so-called emerging markets: Brazil, China, India, Mexico, South Korea and in the resource-rich countries, America, Australia, Canada and New Zealand. Although Britain can and does trade with these countries, European regulation prevents the UK from making trade and investment deals which lower trade barriers and reduce tariffs, i.e., the EU stops the UK from forming a customs union. This is because European countries would see an additional customs union as unfair competition.[7]

Neoliberalism & its consequences

The above three reasons coalesced at the right time for Britain's policymaking elite. They want to pursue neoliberalism in the face of a more reluctant Europe. The word neoliberal is a portmanteau of neo (new) and liberal. It is a propaganda term referring to a 19th century economic model in which government refrains from intervening in markets ('small government') and allows the nature of the market to take its course. It is also known as *laissez-faire*, from the French, let people do as they choose. In the historic sense, 'people' or 'persons' refers to corporations (hence corporate personhood). The theory is that by deregulating, the wealth acquired from trade, investments, mergers, and acquisitions, will trickle down to the working classes and spread.[8]

In the real-world, 'neoliberalism' amounts to socialism for the rich and capitalism for the poor. A prime example of this is the Financial Crisis 2008. After a series of deregulations beginning in the 1970s and peaking in the 1990s, the financial institutions in Wall Street and London – advisers, asset firms, banks, building societies, hedge funds, insurers, liquidity companies and pensions firms – made riskier and riskier decisions (*laissez-faire*). When their artificial bubbles of credit, junk bonds and toxic assets collapsed, the taxpayer had to step in and bail them out under a series of government insurance policies (corporate socialism).[9]

Since these kind of neoliberal programmes were adopted

by successive governments in the US and UK in the 1970s, '80s, and '90s, the gap between rich and poor has widened to the point where Britain hosted 120 billionaires by the year 2015, compared with 5.1 million social security claimants. In most years from the end of WWII to the 1970s, unemployment was under 3%. In 1971, it rose to 3.5% and by 1986 was 11.8%. Further fluctuations correlate with neoliberal policies, wage stagnation for lower- and middle-income earners, and the sell-off of state assets, including water, telecoms, rail and energy services.[10]

In the 1980s and 1990s, neoliberalism infected the political ideology of the European Economic Community. In a report for the London School of Economics, Professor of Law Bojan Bugarič writes that left-wing governments in the EU became more centrist. This paved the way for a more neoliberal-orientated EU. As noted, these policies were already deeply rooted in the US and the UK. The Single European Act 1986 and the Maastricht Treaty 1992 'were the consequence[s] of a broad political convergence among the key member states (Germany, France and Britain) towards the neoliberal goal of creating a single European market', writes Bugarič. 'The relaunching of European integration thus coincided with a major shift in the political ideology. The golden age of the Keynesian welfare state' — referring to the socialist economist John Maynard Keynes — 'did come to an end and gave its way to a new powerful ideology — pro-market neoliberalism'.[11]

Professor Mark Pollack writes that during the 1980s, France, Germany and the UK 'embraced the neoliberal goal of a single European market, which would provide Europe with the economies of scale necessary to compete against the rival economies of the United States and Japan'. Obviously,

America didn't want that to happen. Pollack concludes that '[i]t was in this context of neoliberal consensus' that European Commission President, Jacques Delors, proposed the 1992 programme, which eventually created the single currency, 'together with a series of institutional reforms designed to facilitate the rapid adoption of the Commission's proposed Directives'.[12]

Political scientists Bohrer and Tan note that even before the Financial Crisis 2008, Maastricht 'brought austerity across the member states, in spite of high levels of unemployment in the region'. It mattered not that left-wing governments held 13 out of 15 positions: the governments were hamstrung by Brussels' policies, except the UK, which refused to sign up to the Economic Monetary Union. Proving that they can punish their populations sufficiently with austerity, eleven countries were subsequently admitted to the Economic Monetary Union, eventually adopting the euro. These measures were particularly cruel in light of the recession hitting Europe at the time. Germany's unemployment, for instance, was worse than at any time since the 1930s. Bohrer and Tan spoke of the 'austerity *required* by the Maastricht criteria' (emphasis added), with governments 'unable (or unwilling) to stem the tide of unemployment by expensive propositions such as expanding the public sector'. They note the European Union's 'general retrenchment of welfare state benefits ... as countries seek to remain in the acceptable deficit and debt zones'.[13]

Who voted Brexit & why
Britons from the working classes who voted Leave did so because they want *less* neoliberalism. The mega-rich (multi-millionaires and billionaires) who voted Leave did so because

they want *more* neoliberalism. So, how did the two get married? The latter succeeded in turning the former against their own interests by blaming immigrants and Brussels' technocrats for the consequences of neoliberalism: economic downturn, job insecurity and declining life quality. Leaving the EU, they said, will solve the problem. This short book documents the likelihood that, given the nature of the neoliberal project, the reverse is true: there will be more competition, more immigration and more privatization.[14]

There will also be more globalization. Globalization means different things to different people. In the propaganda sense, globalization means trading with different countries to maximize choice, minimize cost and boost employment. In the real sense, globalization means asset stripping foreign countries (particularly of their raw materials and public services), using the skills of foreigners instead of the skills of domestic workers and putting domestic labourers in competition with exploited workers overseas. The withdrawal from the European Union has led many to believe that the age of globalization is at an end, at least for the time; that countries are becoming more isolated. Isolation would imply the use of domestic resources, including skilled labour. As this short book documents, there will in fact be more globalization and less isolation, as Britain seeks to exploit the emerging markets.[15]

The Lord Ashcroft polls surveyed over 12,000 individuals in the run-up to the referendum.

Many who voted Leave have blamed the EU, rightly or wrongly, for their status in life. The following percentages of Leavers said the following forces were bad for them and their standard of life: multiculturalism 81% (compared with 19% of those who voted Remain), social liberalism 80% (20% Remain), feminism 74% (26% Remain), the Green movement 78% (31% Remain), globalization 69% (31% Remain), the internet 71% (29% Remain), capitalism 51% (49% Remain) and immigration 80% (20% Remain). 22% of Remainers said that working hard enables success, regardless of background, compared with just 16% of vote Leavers. This shows how hard-hit the Leave camp felt with regards to their work-life prospects. 42% of Leavers agreed that the future will threaten their standard of living, compared with 20% of Remainers. 71% of Leavers said their standard of living was under threat, compared to 29% of Remainers. 43% of Remainers said the 'economy, jobs and prices' were a reason for staying.[16]

Many people believe that voting Leave will help the UK regain its sovereignty from the clutches of Brussels' bureaucrats. 31% of Remainers agreed that the UK has not sacrificed sovereignty on what they regard as core issues, like the euro and Schengen system of free movement (more on which later). They said that the UK enjoys 'the best of both worlds' by retaining sovereignty over its currency and levels of migration, while staying in the Union. 9% cited cultural and historical reasons for staying in, and 17% said they didn't want to be isolated from European friends and neighbours. Among the public, 58% of Tories voted Leave, even though their party's position was Remain. Most of the mega-rich, described in Chapter 1, are Tory donors. They pushed for Brexit. Only 37% of Labour voters voted to Leave, as did 30% of Liberal Democrats. Unsurprisingly, 96% of UKIP voters voted Leave. 25% of Greens voted to Leave, as did 36% of Scottish National Party voters.[17]

In Chapter 1, we document who sponsored the Leave propaganda campaign. Project Fear was a nickname given by Leavers to the government's Remain propaganda, which said that the sky would fall if Britain voted to Leave. Interestingly, 39% of Remainers compared with 36% of Leavers said they had 'always known' how they would vote. This indicates that most people could have been swayed either way. Remain's Project Fear turned a lot of people off, possibly swaying them to Leave.[18]

Age, status, religion and ethnicity also played a role.

According to the Lord Ashcroft polls, 73% of 18–24-year-olds voted Remain, as did 62% of 25–34-year-olds. 'Most people with children aged ten or under voted to remain; most of those with children aged 11 or older voted to leave'. Interestingly, the year's age difference coincides with migrants from Poland and Romania seeking work in the UK as a result of British migration policy following the accession of Poland to the EU in 2004. Those parents with older children would have been deluged with anti-migrant propaganda by the media post-2004.

The majority of full- and part-time employed voted Remain, with the majority of unemployed voting Leave. Over half of those on a private pension voted Leave, 'as did two thirds of those retired on a state pension'. Here, poverty is a clear factor. Two thirds of housing association and council tenants voted Leave. A small majority of private renters and mortgage payers voted Remain, indicating that the higher up the income chain, the more likely a Remain vote. Most home-owners, however, voted to Leave.[19]

Education was also a factor. 57% of persons with a university degree voted Remain. 64% of those with a higher degree and 81% of those in full-time education voted Remain. A slight majority of white people voted Leave: 53%. 67% of self-described Asians voted Remain, 'as did three quarters (73%) of black voters'. 70% of Muslims voted Remain, compared with 58% Christians who voted Leave. The only clear majority for Remain was among professionals and managers (57%), again showing that those who haven't done too badly out of neoliberalism are more likely to want to stay.[20]

A split in the hierarchy

Most businesses were in favour of Remain. Why, then, did their campaign fail? There are three answers to this question. They have to do with the nature of the hierarchy in which businesses operate.

Number one: we should not think of big business as a monolith pursuing exactly the same goals. There are, to be sure, common goals: among them, cost minimization and profit maximization. These have complicated effects on workers and the broader economy. There are also divergent interests. Proprietary banks — banks that use internal funds to play the markets — consider hedge funds to be a rival because they conduct similar operations. Both hedge funds and banks abhor regulation, but banks can be adversely affected by financial volatility caused by hedge funds and their gambling. Hedge funds, conversely, thrive on volatility and market instability.[21]

Hedge funds can make individuals extremely wealthy. In this short book, we call these individuals the mega-rich. They sit at the top of the economic hierarchy. Their wealth enables them to push for policies that might be against the interests of other big businesses, including banks, drug companies, the energy industry and so on. We call the CEOs in the latter group the super-rich. However, even among hedge fund CEOs there was division on the Brexit question.

Number two: staying in Europe wasn't a life or death decision for most businesses. Even though it is a financial and regulatory inconvenience for most businesses to Leave the European Union, markets are so internationalized – i.e., traded in and backed by the dollar – the weakened pound resulting from Brexit actually benefited Britain's most profitable businesses. This is because it made their products more affordable on the international market. This in turn boosted exports. Big business must have anticipated a weakened pound and rise in exports and did not therefore panic too much over the hedge funds' push for Brexit. Indeed, most of the pro-Remain donors and representatives were politicians, not big business representatives. However, even within big business there were some elements who wanted to Leave, even though their own companies' official position was Remain (see Chapter 1). This only serves to highlight the complexity and divisiveness of the issue.[22]

Number three: powerful internationalist elements of the government decided that Britain wasn't making enough of the opportunities out there in Commonwealth countries and across Asia and South America. Exactly what percentage of the Conservative government – including the shadow state of PR people, private donors, business–government liaison officers, and revolving door think tank advisors – wanted to Leave and what percentage wanted to Remain is impossible to say. One thing we can be sure of, however, is that as soon as PM Cameron stepped down, PM May's cabinet was filled with Eurosceptic internationalists, as we document later. Backed by the US, whose official position was that Britain should Remain part of the European Union, and by certain hedge fund CEOs, the apparent minority of Brexiteers in the Tory government became unusually powerful, as their immediate appointments to various cabinet positions demonstrates.[23]

Introduction

What is the European Union and what influence does it have over Whitehall? This Introduction demonstrates that, contrary to popular belief, Britain retained a great deal of sovereignty and, what's more, led Europe's neoliberal agenda. Because of economic neoliberalism, the very things that many pro-Leave members of the public voted against — economic uncertainty and high levels of migration, among them — are more than likely to continue and possibly expand under Brexit.

Two political advisors who work for the right-wing, pro-'free market' Heritage Foundation are also members of the Margaret Thatcher Center for Freedom. They have close links to the US and UK right-wing establishment, and represent neoliberal opinion. Two years before Brexit — which they strongly advocated — they wrote that, '[b]etween 1946 and 1989, the U.S. promoted closer cooperation between the European democracies, seeing this closeness as an economic and political contribution to winning the Cold War'. The authors go on to note that, '[a]fter the Cold War was conclusively over, the policy of European integration was no longer in the U.S. interest'.[1]

This coincided with Anglo-American efforts to push 'free trade' on Europe, with for instance the Treaty of Maastricht, and to further open the EU economy to the US, which eventually led to the disastrous Financial Crisis 2008 and its awful austerity aftermath.

Strange bedfellows

The Brexit debates made for strange political bedfellows indeed. Nigel Farage is an ex-Tory who used to work in finance (credit and stocks). Farage went on to lead the UK Independence Party and, in the general election campaign of 2015, said live on television that non-Britons should not receive AIDS treatment in the UK. On the Brexit issue, Farage sat on the same side of the fence – Leave – as, for example, Tariq Ali: a prominent left-wing socialist writer, editor and activist. Farage said that British businesses and thus workers would be stronger out of Europe and its regulations. Ali argued that Brexit would constrain *Europe's* neoliberal effect on Britain (as opposed to Britain's neoliberal effect on Europe).[2]

Likewise, self-professed socialist, Owen Jones, shared a Remain seat with his nemesis, David Cameron, the Tory Prime Minister. While Farage was merely threatening to speed up the deaths of AIDS victims by denying them treatment, under Cameron's leadership thousands of social security recipients actually perished when their meagre benefits were stopped as part of the government's attack on the poor. This was heavily criticized by Jones, to give one example of their political differences. Both Cameron and Jones separately argued that Britain would be better off Remaining.[3]

Nobody suggested a more nuanced approach to Brexit, such as retaining the EU's directives to protect workers' rights while eliminating the articles of the Treaty of Rome 1993 which enable member states to privatize social services and state assets. Instead, the public was given a dialectical in-out option, both in the way in which the debate was framed and in the choice of the given outcome.[4]

After the referendum, pundits in the alternative media were euphoric about the result. For years they had been speaking out against the New World Order: a US-led project to create a one-world government. They saw the European Union solely in this context, a region of world-government, and not, from America's perspective, as a useful short-term bloc against Soviet expansion. For the alternative media, and justly so, the final straw against the European Union was its handling of the post-financial crisis. Since 2009, the European Central Bank and the European Commission, under the advice of the rulers (not internal economists) of the International Monetary Fund, imposed brutal austerity across Europe, with Greece being the most visible victim.[5]

For the alternative media, Brexit represented 'people power': an active opposition to global forces hell-bent on micromanaging every aspect of our lives. While there is truth to this narrative, it overlooks the bigger picture: neoliberal internationalism, which is dealt with in Chapters 2 and 3 of this short book.

What are we leaving?
Many people on the left and right, in the mainstream and in the alternative media, believe that Brexit means a return to British sovereignty. In fact, many of the neoliberal programmes that Britain has adopted over the last four decades were adopted outside the framework of the EU. Furthermore, Britain's stubbornness precluded its total surrender to Brussels.[6]

Britain has been described by scholars of European law as an 'awkward partner'. It never adopted the euro, never agreed to the Schengen system of free movement of people and never signed the Fundamental Charter of Human Rights. Britain holds a record number of opt-outs. To what extent, then, does EU law affect British sovereignty? Technically, Brussels has sovereignty over British law. The issue was formally settled between 1989 and 2000. Under the Merchant Shipping Act 1988 (MSA), UK fishing vessels had to be owned up to 75% by Britons or British-registered companies. The European Court of Justice ruled that the MSA was contrary to EU law as it denied the principle of a Single Market. In *Factortame Ltd vs. Secretary of State for Transport* (various cases between 1989 to 2000), the House of Lords decreed the supremacy of EU law over British law and sovereignty. While this is true on paper, in reality EU sovereignty over UK policy decisions is largely a fantasy.[7]

For instance, although the Blair government opted-in to the Maastricht Treaty's chapter on pay and health and safety, domestically it dismantled many of these protections. Protocol 25 of the Maastricht Treaty left monetary policy with the British government, hence the fallacy of blaming austerity in the UK on the European Central Bank and the European System of Central Banks: it was a Tory policy, used as an excuse to privatize services. In the wake of crippling Troika-imposed austerity that left children going hungry at school, the Greeks on the other hand had a perfectly legitimate reason for wanting out of the EU.[8]

On fiscal and monetary policy, the Bank of England injected useless cash into the economy to stop the pound from getting overvalued (quantitative easing) before the

Eurozone countries did the same. Opting out of the Stability and Growth Pact, which caps public deficits (at 3% of GDP), Britain runs some of the highest deficits in Europe.[9]

Protocol 36 of the Lisbon Treaty allows the UK to opt-out of justice and home affairs (JHA) legislation (broadly known as Title V legislation). The UK's so-called block opt-out from all JHA legislation that came into force prior to Lisbon, included 130 measures. It was a choice of the incumbent Cameron Tory government to opt-in to 35 measures in 2014, including the European Arrest Warrant and Europol. Home Secretary and future PM Theresa May accused the EU of trying to pass legislation under different titles and chapters to circumvent the UK's opt-outs, even though the House of Lords found no evidence to support it.[10]

A report by the Royal Institute of International Affairs points out that 'the UK ... retains sovereignty over its monetary policy'. This includes a deal in February 2016, which sought to limit the European Central Bank's jurisdiction over non-Eurozone countries, retaining the Bank of England's control over domestic fiscal and monetary policy. The deal also opted out of the use of the European Court of Justice's commitment to foster 'closer union among the peoples of Europe' and to extend the political power of Brussels. The European Union Act 2011 commits the British government to holding a referendum on whether to accept EU treaty revisions. In addition, if 55% of a given national parliament votes against EU draft legislation, member state governments cannot vote on it until amendments have been made.[11]

The Chatham House report goes on to say that, 'having decided not to join the Schengen zone', the UK 'exercises sovereign supervision of its borders'. This includes 'the right to deny entry to non-EU citizens arriving from the EU's Schengen area and to EU citizens', if they pose an alleged, arbitrary threat to UK security. The UK retains opt-outs from the EU's common asylum policy and sovereignty over domestic policing, except voluntary agreements over the EU Arrest Warrant and Schengen Information System. Until the rise of ISIS – so convenient for warmongers – the UK was largely split from Europe on its foreign policy, which it aggressively pursued with the US in the Middle East, North Africa and Central Asia.[12]

How does EU membership affect Britain's ability to form free trade deals with other countries?

Cambridge specialist on European Union Law Dr Markus Gehring writes that the EU applies mixed-agreement Free Trade Agreements, from which Britain 'already derives benefits' because of its EU membership. But as the UK is not party to them until all Member States have ratified the agreements, it has to wait. This applies to EU-negotiated agreements with Colombia, Peru, the Caribbean and other countries and regions, including southern African states.

According to Ruth Lea, a post-Brexit Britain would opt for neither the Norway option (i.e., inclusion in the Single Market) nor the Swiss option (exclusion from the Single Market in place of reliance on bilateral agreements). Rather, Britain would seek to negotiate a tariff-free Free Trade Agreement, avoiding the EU's Common External Tariff. There would, crucially, be an agreement on regulatory equivalence for the all-important City of London Corporation's financial services sector, which constitutes nearly 10% of GDP.[13]

How Europe constrains UK trade

In a nutshell: after Britain started deregulating its economy in the early-1970s, it joined the European Economic Community (later known as the EU). While France retained capital controls, Britain tried to push 'free market' doctrines on the EU's customs union, succeeding in the early-1990s with the Maastricht Treaty. The rest of the world hardly mattered because its GDP was comparatively low. However, in the 1980s and '90s, the USA succeeded in pushing free markets on China, India, Mexico and Russia. As a result, those countries' GDPs increased enormously, though the majority of the population of each country saw hardly any of the benefits. After the Financial Crisis 2008, Europe's growth slowed.[14]

As we document in chapters 2 and 3, powerful internationalists have pointed to declining UK-EU trade and the need to back away from Brussels and exploit markets in the rest of the world.

'Since the late 1960s the EU successively assumed the exclusive competence over what it calls the common commercial policy, i.e. international trade', writes European law scholar, Gehring. 'This EU power does not concern purely commercial deals, like the sale of British trains to India', Gehring continues: 'that remains the power of each Member State. Rather the EU power over trade deals concerns general policies like the tariffs (border taxes on imports) and government regulation that might be a barrier to trade'.[15]

The EU is defined under World Trade Organization rules as a customs union, says Gehring. This means that EU member states are not permitted to make trade deals with other countries. Unlike deals such as the North American

Free Trade Agreement, the EU being a customs union does not permit members to set their own tariffs. Gehring writes that the UK could sign more deals with countries if it left the EU, as the EU has trade agreements with only 50 countries. Without EU protection, says Gehring, the UK would face 'pressure' to conclude trade deals like the Transatlantic Trade and Investment Partnership with the USA. This would involve sacrificing public institutions like the National Health Service, which third countries would expect to be opened to privatization.[16]

Brexiteer and Arbuthnot Banking Group advisor Ruth Lea, CBE, writes for the London School of Economics: 'the straightjacket of the EU's Customs Union ... prevents us from bilaterally negotiating treaties' with third countries. Currently over 60% of Britain's exports are with the EU and USA (44.4% and 17.1%, respectively). After that, the UK's biggest exports go to Switzerland, China, the Arab Gulf States and Japan. The growing markets of Australia, Canada, India, Norway, Russia, Singapore and Saudi Arabia come second. Britain's free marketeers wanted to quit the EU and capture these markets. Unlike the EU, the European Free Trade Agreement has regional trade agreements with Canada, Hong Kong, Singapore and South Korea. It is negotiating agreements with Belarus, Kazakhstan, and Russia.[17]

'Is our net £10 billion contribution to the EU a price worth paying for tariff-free access to the EU market?', asks Tory ex-Trade Secretary, Peter Lilley. Eurosceptic Lilley used to work for W. Greenwell & Co. stockbrokers and, as Secretary of State at the Department of Social Security, lampooned Gilbert and Sullivan's song The Mikado, in which Lilley rhapsodized about 'sponging socialists'. In the 1990s, he opposed the

Major government's signing of Maastricht without a referendum. 'If we left the EU with no trade deal ... our exports would face EU tariffs averaging just 2.4 per cent', wrote Lilley shortly before the June 2016 referendum. Lilley explains that 'our net contribution to the EU budget is equivalent to a 7 per cent tariff'. Therefore, it's cheaper to dump the EU and trade 'with fast-growing developing countries which still have high tariffs'.[18]

The hope will be in bilateral agreements, or those worked out through the supranational World Trade Organization. Membership of the EU prevents the UK from independently negotiating 'free trade' deals, and the agreements made by the EU on the UK's behalf have excluded Australia, Brazil, China and India. Lilley then goes on to note that under the legal 'principle of continuity', Britain would be entitled to 'adapt' EU treaties to the UK and continue trading in the Single Market, as does 'every country' that chooses to do so. Later, we quote government documents confirming their desire to expand the Single Market – presumably to include Australia, Brazil, etc. – while simultaneously backing away from the constraints of Europe. This is called having your cake and eating it.[19]

More migrants

According to the Royal Institute of International Affairs in its report on UK sovereignty, the 'pooling of sovereign power' was of little concern to the British public except after 2004, with the EU's enlargement, which meant that higher numbers of eastern European migrants came to the UK, with 65,000 net migrants coming to the UK in 2012 and 172,000 in 2015: most of whom were from Poland.[20]

The Eurozone is open to non-EU members. The European Economic Area is contingent on countries joining the European Free Trade Association (EFTA), of which Iceland, Lichtenstein, Norway and Switzerland are members. Britain was a founding member of the EFTA in 1960, but quit in 1973 to accede (initially without a referendum) to the European Economic Community (later EU). Britain will have to rejoin the EFTA if it wants continued access to the Single Market (the 'Norway deal'). Those who wanted a Brexit based on concerns about immigration will be angry, as the EFTA guarantees the free movement of people.[21]

Brexit is politically dominated by free marketeers. Open Europe is a think tank committed to '[r]egulat[ing] business less'. It has published several reports on Brexit, including one co-authored by Raoul Ruparel of the British Chamber of Commerce. The report concludes that Britain can only benefit in the wake of Brexit if it pursues deregulation. '[T]he path to prosperity outside the EU lies through: free trade and opening up to low cost competition, maintaining a relatively high immigration (albeit with a different mix of skills), and pushing through deregulation and economic reforms'. The report says: 'There is no doubt that such an approach would disappoint a number of people on the "Leave" side'. It adds: 'there are several reasons why we believe headline net immigration is unlikely to reduce much', the main one being, '[t]he business case for maintaining a flexible supply of labour'.[22]

Notice that despite claims of supporting a Northern Powerhouse initiative – to get the de-industrialized north of England back as an industrial centre – none of the government studies or free-market think tanks are proposing education programmes to teach manufacturing, production and design skills to Britons. Rather, they are looking to use, for example, Chinese designers, Mexican manufacturers and migrant producers. The Open Europe study goes on to say that, 'free from EU rules on free movement, the UK would likely pursue a selective policy more geared towards attracting skilled migration'. Forced to work on temporary visas, Burmese engineers, for example, can be more economically efficient to hire (i.e., cheaper) than their Western European counterparts, who retain at least some rights under EU law.[23]

The points-based system of Australia and Canada could be adopted in the UK with regards to immigration. 'Such a system could give priority to UK industries and employers suffering skills shortages but also allow a flexible supply of workers to enter the UK labour force'.[24]

Chapter 1

The Mega-Rich

This chapter tells of how a small number of very rich, very influential CEOs from hedge funds and other financial services decided to cut the weak regulatory shackles of Europe and make themselves and their companies even richer by targeting foreign markets. They donated to the Tory party in the run up to the Brexit referendum and were influential in promoting various Leave groups.

The post-war economy: 'The managerial aristocracy'

Between the end of WWII and the early-1970s, there were no major economic crises or recessions in the UK or America, except brief periods in 1956 and 1961 in the UK. Public spending on national industry, health, insurance and social security led to a 50% increase in wages for the young working classes. Within ten years, Britain's huge post-war debt had reduced substantially. There was a problem, however: wealth was more equally distributed, with the working classes taking a share of the upper-classes' profits. To stop this unwanted development, the upper-classes in the US and Britain arranged for a series of financial deregulations, which started significantly under Nixon in the 1970s and were put into overdrive under Reagan and Thatcher in the 1980s.[1]

This was known as economic neoliberalism, or free market economics.

In 1971, the Bank of England created the Competition and Credit Control (C&CC) mechanism. This meant the end of state-control over worthless credit growth. Whereas post-war credit and loans had been put into the 'real economy' of houses, cars, production, etc., it was now the privilege of the bloated financial sector. '[T]he brakes were well and truly off... Just take your wheelbarrow to the banks and cart away the cash', said Edward Du Cann MP, then Chair of Keysers bank. 'These immediate years after C&CC were wonderful shovelling times', said Charles Gordon of Cedar Holdings. The result was the increase in domestic interest rates to offset the issuance of credit.[2]

Another consequence of so-called economic deregulation was the growth of the financial services sector: asset managers, building societies, equity firms, insurance and reinsurance, liquidity providers, pensions companies and hedge funds. Hedge funds are companies that use credit and/ or borrowed capital to make risky investments. There are now 600 hedge funds in the City of London Corporation, managing $472bn, or two-thirds of Europe's hedge fund assets, according to Preqin.[3]

Since the 1980s, 'incomes have risen for the top 0.1% even faster than the top 1%', writes Jonathan Cribb of the Institute for Fiscal Studies (IFS). The standard measure of economic inequality in the UK is the Gini coefficient, set between 0 and 1. According to IFS, income inequality was 0.25 in 1979 and 0.34 in 1991, having 'increased rapidly in the 1980s'. Not considered by Cribb is the causal relation between economic deregulation and poverty. Cribb writes that by 1979, the top 10% had an income 1.8 times higher than half the population. '[W]ithin the top 1%, the incomes of the richest had grown fastest'. By 2011, median salaries were £26,000 per annum. However, only the top 10% earn(ed) over £52,600 a year. Europe was not as keen to adopt neoliberalism, with France retaining capital controls into the 1980s. Australia, New Zealand, Britain and the USA have experienced comparable internal wealth inequality, whereas 'most continental European countries' have avoided such a sharp trend.[4]

Liquidity provider Citigroup refers to Australia, Canada, the USA and Britain as plutonomy economies, where the top 1% has as much wealth as the bottom 90%. Two leaked investment advice papers refer to financial institutions as the 'Managerial Aristocracy'. They go on to note that unaffordable living costs, especially in the housing sector, will likely buoy the top 1%, who stimulate the services economy by buying luxury goods, such as cars, cosmetics, cruises, fashions, jewellery, etc. 'Society and governments need to be amenable to disproportionately allow/encourage the few to retain that fatter profit share. The Managerial Aristocracy ... needs to commandeer a vast chunk of that rising profit share, either through capital income, or simply paying itself a lot', the advisers explain.[5]

After the crisis: 'Full liberalisation'
Deregulation is largely to blame for the Financial Crisis 2008 in the USA, which, due to the interconnectedness of markets, especially in the gilts and bonds sectors, sent shockwaves across Europe. In response, the Troika – the UN's International Monetary Fund, the European Central Bank and the European Commission – recommended brutal austerity, despite warnings from many of their own economists that social spending was the way out of recession. Austerity was

an excuse to expand privatization. In the UK, which had no IMF debts and did not adopt the euro, austerity was a policy choice made in Whitehall, not Brussels.[6]

In response to public pressure, including riots in London, Paris and Athens, the European Parliament and Commission adopted a number of directives to restrain the damaging actions of financial institutions. These were weak, but strong enough to raise objections in London.[7]

The European Commission adopted two Acts to expand the Single Market (2011 and 2012). The Acts sought to end 'market fragmentation' and increase the internal market. This posed a problem to the political establishment of Britain because fragmentation, particularly where investment flows are concerned, is of immense benefit. If the UK had to follow the rules established by the European Central Bank, the government would have poured less public money into bailing out the financial institutions that caused the crisis. '[P]rotectionism is no longer respectable as a policy position within Europe', says the British government in its review of the Single Market. The Commission also decided to strengthen the Economic and Monetary Union, which the British government said could 'weaken the collective commitment of all member states to maintain and deepen market liberalisation and competition. It could put non-euro area countries', like the UK and its allies, 'at a competitive disadvantage'.[8]

The European Banking Authority sought to regulate financial service providers across the EU, including those like the UK not inside the Eurozone. The UK objected to this and managed to prevent the Commission from gaining a Eurozone majority. Despite this, the British government feared that 'it might generate pressure to extend this tighter regime to non-euro area countries to prevent euro area economies being undercut', says the government's review. 'All this means that safeguards to preserve the Single Market and the rights of Euro "outs" within it could well be necessary in the coming years'. The report, published in 2012, goes on to state that 'further deepening of the Single Market would produce economic gains. Full liberalisation of all areas where there are significant non-tariff barriers could increase EU GDP by 14% and UK GDP by 7%'. In other words, the Tory government wanted to pursue free markets across a reluctant EU. '[T]o achieve that would require a major drive on both legislation and enforcement, largely in areas which have so far proved resistant to liberalisation for political reasons. There is little sign that this is possible'. The Tory government felt that Brexit might be a viable option.[9]

The European Securities and Markets Authority (ESMA) describes the EU's Markets in Financial Instruments Directive (MIFID), which came into force just before the financial crisis, as aiming to create 'a single market for investment services and activities and to ensure a high degree of harmonised protection for investors and financial instruments'. This was bad news for the City of London's financial institutions because they feared losing their operational sovereignty in the Brussels' bureaucracy. MIFID was expanded by MIFID II, which 'aims at specifying, in particular, the rules relating to determining liquidity for equity instruments, the rules on the provision of market data on a reasonable commercial basis, the rules on publication, order execution and transparency obligations for systematic internalisers', and so on.[10]

Until the Alternative Investment Fund Managers Directive (AIFMD) was adopted by the European Parliament and Council in 2011, little harmonized EU regulation existed on collective investment schemes, except the Undertakings for Collective Investment in Transferable Securities Directive. The AIFMD 'provides many challenges to the alternative investment fund industry', says a TaylorWessing legal analysis. Crucially, 'it is not the fund that is regulated by the AIFMD, only the manager of the fund'. This sent CEOs reeling at the possibility of facing personal sanctions.[11]

According to the *Independent*, a KPMG survey expected a rise in costs of 5% to hedge funds due to the legislation, 'which is probably going to be passed on to investors'. The transfer of cost from investors instead of taxpayers is bad for CEOs because investors can use their corporate democratic privileges to vote out unpopular CEOs. The AIFMD requires 'managers to obtain authorisation, meet on-going operating conditions and comply with transparency and reporting requirements', says corporate surveyors, PwC.[12]

The backlash: 'Turbo-charging free trade'

The Tories had been backing away from Europe for years. One of the problems was the EU's financial transactions tax, which the UK challenged on account of its hurting Britain's most lucrative schemes: financial services exports. As then-Mayor and future Foreign Secretary Boris Johnson said: 'We cannot allow jobs, growth and livelihoods to be jeopardized by those in the EU who mistakenly view financial services as an easy target'. Jobs refers to the millionaires and multi-millionaires in the financial services sector. Growth refers to macroeconomic growth, the vast chunk of which goes into the pockets of the wealthy and amounts to little more than speculative bubbles for the broader economy. And livelihoods refers to the millions of pounds made by CEOs.[13]

In the UK general election 2010, the Liberal Democrats betrayed their voters by joining with the Tories, who did not win an out-right majority in Parliament. The Coalition Agreement between the Tories and the Liberals published in 2010 states: 'Britain should play a leading role in an enlarged European Union', but crucially doesn't say what the role should be. Rather, 'no further powers should be transferred to Brussels without a referendum'. Over the five years of Tory/Liberal government, Britain, meaning the establishment, vowed to 'protect [...] national sovereignty'. In a blow to working people, the coalition also vowed 'to limit the application of the [EU's] Working Time Directive in the United Kingdom'. The Coalition Agreement also committed the government to drafting a so-called United Kingdom Sovereignty Bill, 'to make it clear that ultimate authority remains with Parliament'. This is in contrast to the European Communities Act 1972 and the Lords' ruling on sovereignty.[14]

Indeed, the final draft bill, *United Kingdom Borders (Control and Sovereignty) Bill* is described as 'provision for the re-establishment of the control and sovereignty of policy, administration and all other matters relating to the United Kingdom's borders with the European Union and to the entry and exit to the United Kingdom of foreign nationals; and for connected purposes'. The statement also 'support[s] the further enlargement of the EU' — for other countries, that is. Britain already held a record number of opt-outs from EU law.[15]

In July 2012, the government published its *Review of the Balance of Competences* between the United Kingdom and the European Union. It opens with a statement from the Foreign Secretary, William Hague: 'We are committed to playing a leading role in the European Union in order to advance our national interest'. National interest means the interests of the big business community and the political establishment. '[W]e will continue to push an ambitious programme of deepening the single market while seeking to reduce unnecessary burdens in EU legislation'. The report goes on: 'in the face of a shift of economic power to the emerging markets, the EU needs to be more outward-looking, more dynamic and more competitive on the global stage'.[16]

The Tory manifesto 2015 states that the EU 'is too big, too bossy and too bureaucratic'. This translates as: EU fiscal and monetary policy is impeding Anglo-American capital. On the Transatlantic Trade and Investment Partnership (TTIP), the deal being worked out in secret by the US and EU, the manifesto commits the Tories to 'completing ambitious trade deals and reducing red tape'. Red tape translates as regulations designed to avoid another financial crisis: a crisis which helped garner hatred of Brussels, despite the fact that Britain's austerity was, in reality, largely a Tory policy choice. 'We say: yes to the Single Market. Yes to turbo-charging free trade'.[17]

As the Tories signalled their desire to back away from a slowing, more regulated Europe, certain mega-rich hedge fund managers started donating more money to the Tories, helping to set up the Leave campaign, and signalling that they wanted a Brexit.

The European Commission 'launched an onslaught on

hedge funds', wrote Paul Marshall before Brexit. Worth
£465m, Marshall of Marshall Wace hedge funds explained in
a *Financial Times* article that the Commission 'largely ignored
the issue of bank leverage, focusing instead on hedge fund
[...]' regulation. The draft Alternative Investment Fund
Managers Directive (mentioned above) 'proposed restrictions
on hedge fund leverage, rules on depositories, remuneration,
liquidity, valuation, and protectionist measures'. The idea of
other people making the rules is intolerable to the 'Managerial Aristocracy'. Marshall quotes an anonymous Belgium
MEP who supposedly said that the EC had 'always wanted to
hit' hedge funds, which is hardly surprising, given their role
in the financial crisis, which forced European politicians to
respond, at least in a small way, to the concerns of their
constituents.[18]

Two academics, Jensen and Snaith, wrote a paper for the
Journal of European Public Policy. They found broad support
for Britain remaining in the EU among large businesses and
policymakers, who have made their views known in public
and in print. But in addition to the majority of businesses,
there is 'a powerful minority, mainly comprising hedge funds,
... [which] is in favour of leaving'. There was much secrecy
surrounding the hedge fund Brexit campaign, hence the
authors' reliance on phone conversations with anonymous
sources. The authors conclude that a 'much-touted potential
benefit of leaving the EU would be regulatory easing, as it
would allow the government to roll back costly legislation'.[19]

Academia is not the only place reduced to using anonymous sources. A year before Brexit, the *Independent* quoted an
anonymous hedge fund boss: 'Many are generally opposed to
[the EU]', referring to Euroscepticism among peers. The

paper reports that '[t]wo of the five richest hedge fund billionaires in Britain are already linked to EU exit campaigns, and *The Independent* understands that other fund managers are planning to throw their weight behind the Out campaign in the coming months'. The hedge fund managers cite '[t]ough European rules made in the wake of the 2007 financial crisis'. But these regulations 'would be under threat if hedge fund bosses helped to force the UK's exit from the EU'. Hedge funds would make an additional £250m per annum from Brexit, says the *Independent*.[20]

According to the *Financial Times*, 'Downing Street and senior pro-EU Tory officials have been concerned for some time that wealthy hedge fund figures, many of whom are eurosceptic, could pour money into the Brexit campaign, boosting its resources ahead of a referendum due by 2017', which the Tories decided to hold in 2016, when Euroscepticism was rife among the electorate, many of whom had been conditioned to believe that Brussels, not Whitehall and the City of London Corporation, was the source of their woes.[21]

Not all sources quote anonymous traders. George Soros, the multibillionaire speculator, caused a crisis of confidence in the British pound in 1992 by betting on its devaluation. Soros bragged: 'I was fortunate enough to make a substantial profit for my hedge fund investors, at the expense of the Bank of England and the British government'. On Brexit, he said 'there are speculative forces in the markets much bigger and more powerful' than proprietary banks. 'And they will be eager to exploit any miscalculations by the British government or British voters'. Soros is one of them. He allegedly made millions buying gold – a so-called safe market – before Brexit, though his official position was Remain.[22]

The mega-rich

According to the *Wall Street Journal*, UK-based hedge funds 'keep an ultralow profile'. They make up 70% to 80% of the EU's hedge-fund assets, making London the hedge fund capital of Europe. Hedge funds have 'wealthy owners who are politically active', putting the pro-Remain bankers and medium- to large-businesses at a disadvantage.[23]

Peter Hargeaves is reportedly worth £1bn and is co-founder of Hargreaves Lansdown, a financial services buyer and seller. He gave the Leave.EU campaign its biggest contribution: £3.2m.[24]

Peter Cruddas is reportedly the richest man in London, worth over £1bn. Cruddas was the Conservative Party's co-treasurer and founder of CMC Markets. He has stated that he donated over £1m to the Tory party. 'Anti-EU supporters from the spread betting industry include Peter Cruddas ... and Stuart Wheeler, the founder of rival spread betting firm IG Group', says the *Guardian* in an article published a year before Brexit.[25]

Worth over £40m, Wheeler is a former barrister-cum-investment banker. He was a major Tory donor until he shifted to UKIP in 2011. Wheeler had backed ministers Liam Fox and David Davis – both Eurosceptics – for Tory leaders against Cameron, whom he criticized for his stance on the Treaty of Lisbon. In 2008, he sued the Labour government for its ratification of the Lisbon Treaty without a referendum. 'Hedge funds like ... market volatility', the pre-Brexit *Guardian* report continues. Morgan Stanley anticipated a 20% drop in the FTSE from Brexit. 'In the hedge fund industry based in London's Mayfair, that prospect has profit potential', the report explains, because hedge funds spread their risks and profit from downturn. The hedge fund class has 'a dislike for what they regard as overburdensome – and profit-reducing – regulation'.[26]

Born in China, Sir Michael Hintze is a British-Australian businessman, reported by *Forbes* to be worth $1.8bn. He is a major patron of the Tory party and a banker for the Pope. In New York, he worked for the Salomon Brothers and Credit Suisse First Boston. He then became the head of equity trading at Goldman Sachs. In 1999, Hintze formed the hedge fund CQS Asset Management. Hintze manages $11bn of assets. Interestingly, Hintze, who was knighted in 2013, has made a number of personal donations to many ministers who ended up in Theresa May's Eurosceptic cabinet, including Davis (future Brexit Minister), Fox (Trade Sec.), Boris Johnson (Foreign Sec.) and May herself. Hintze also advises the think tank Business for Britain.[27]

According to the *Financial Times*, Hintze has given £3.2m to the Tories over the last decade. In the year running up to Brexit, he was said by colleagues to be ' "considering" a generous donation'. Although there is no evidence that Hintze directly donated to the Tories over Brexit or directly funded a Leave campaign, a friend said: 'I think he is almost certain to donate, it is a cause he is passionate about'. Hintze's son, John, was reportedly tasked with researching for the Vote Leave campaign, which donated the second largest sum to the overall Leave movement.[28]

Crispin Odey is worth an estimated £900m. He manages the hedge fund Odey Asset Management, which manages £6.5bn. He states that hedge funds are not monolithic, and many wished to stay in Europe. The pro-Remainers include David Harding of Winton Capital Management, Ewan Kirk of

Cantab Capital Partners, Andrew Law of Caxton Associates and Manny Roman of Man Group. Through the so-called Democracy Movement and Global Britain Ltd, Odey donated over £520,000 to the broad Leave campaign, which he described as 'not much'.[29]

Tosca Fund asset managements, founded by Martin Hughes and worth $4bn, backed Brexit and said that the EU turned from a 'much needed economic union to one with unwelcome political ambitions', like those mentioned: namely regulation. The author of the Tosca Fund Brexit report, Dr Savvas Savouri, says that China is the largest single market for cars built in Britain. Savouri writes, 'Britain is very much a flourishing economy as much of Europe is floundering'.[30]

Worth £150m, Michael Baron Farmer, or Mr Copper as he is known on account of his long-term investments in the eponymous metal trade, formed the Red Kite Hedge (worth $2.3bn) and Mine Finance Group. He is senior treasurer of the Tory party. Farmer gave £200,000 to Vote Leave and said: 'if we all wake up on the 24th [of June]', the day after referendum day, 'and we're still in, there's going to be a grey cloud of depression over this country'.[31]

Eurosceptic and Conservative Party supporter Patrick Barbour founded the Barbour Index, which he sold to a French media group in 1999 for £22m. He donated £500,000 to Vote Leave.[32]

Regulation: 'A genuine threat to financial services'

In the run-up to the referendum, over one thousand business representatives signed a letter expressing their desire to stay in Europe. Their argument is that the Single Market provides a stable source of revenue, that the volatility from leaving would cause a profit loss, and that the ease with which the European Union allows for free travel and geographical indicators, such as Scotch whisky, would be compromised in the wake of a Brexit.[33]

Three hundred representatives signed a letter expressing the opposite sentiment: that as financial service providers (of junk bonds, toxic assets, hedges, etc.), European regulation is hindering their profits. Authored by Dominic Burke of Jardine Lloyd Thompson ((re)insurance), it says: 'We worry that the EU's approach to regulation now poses a genuine threat to our financial services industry and to the competitiveness of the City of London'. They want London to be 'outside the EU but with continued access to its capital markets'. They include: Better Capital (investments), CMC Markets (derivatives), Habib Bank AG Zurich, Hargreaves Lansdown (services), Hiscox Group (insurance), London International Financial Futures and Options Exchange, Marshall Wace (hedge fund), Odey Asset Management (hedge fund), Pakenham Partners (advice), Risk Capital Partners (equity), and Winterflood Securities (liquidity).[34]

What explains the split between Remain and Leave businesses? Edmond de Rothschild writes: 'Proprietary trading by large banks was in direct competition with hedge funds'. Rothschild's institution, 'observed a rise of new fund launches when investment banks closed proprietary trading desks'.[35]

Which side would win, the super-rich or the mega-rich? Internally, there were some divisions, with a former HSBC executive signing the Leave letter. This stood in contrast to HSBC's official Remain position. This one issue alone symbolizes what a polarizing debate Brexit turned out to be; even among those who matter: the super-rich and the mega-rich. Whoever donated the most to their given campaign was a good indication of who would win. Indeed, the Electoral Commission announced that Leave had donated more money to their campaign than Remain had to theirs.[36]

Nearly £16 million was raised by donors by the closing month. Remainers donated £7.4m and Leavers donated £8.1m. The biggest Remain donor was the IN Campaign Ltd, which donated £6.8m. The majority of IN's board of directors included politicians, educators and celebrities. Leavers included the Bruges Group, Grassroots Out (GO), Leave.EU, Vote Leave, WAGTV, and Trade Unionists Against the European Union, which was one of the smallest donors. Vote Leave, whose directors and donors were mainly business-people, donated £2.7m. Leave.EU donated £3.2m. GO donated £2m. GO mainly consisted of politicians. This appears to have given the Leave camp a veneer of political legitimacy. The other pro-Leave groups were blatantly funded by businesspeople. Had the Leave camp consisted solely of businesspeople, the public would have realized what was going on.[37]

Vote Leave's donors included billionaire Cruddas (mentioned above), Martin Bellamy of the Salamanca Group (asset management), Daniel Hodson of LIFFE (an index), Luke Johnson of Risk Capital Partners, Jon Moynihan of PA Consulting, Stuart Wheeler of the IG Index (derivatives) and the Labour Party's biggest individual donor John Mills, chairman of JML. Tory politicians included Liam Fox, Boris Johnson, Priti Patel, Dominic Raab and other internationalist free marketeers, many of whom PM May appointed to her cabinet in foreign policy positions, as we shall see.[38]

Vote Leave's advocates included John Caudwell, a phone entrepreneur and Tory donor, who sold the Caudwell Group to Providence Equity Partners and Doughty Hanson for £1.46bn, allegedly in anticipation of an economic downturn. Vote Leave's advocates also included individuals from or formerly of the Argent Group (food), Business for Sterling (founded Lord Marsh of British Rail), C. Hoare & Co. (bank), Central European Clothing (Tesco), Crispin Odey (hedge fund CEO), Foyles and Noved Investment, Hiscox (insurance), Numis Securities (investment banking), RH Development, Reebok (clothing) and Reliance Security Group ('manpower').[39]

The Leave.EU group is/was led by, among others, Arron Banks (an investor worth £100m and Tory/UKIP donor), Toby Blackwell (publisher), Caroline Drewett (entrepreneur), Jim Mellon (investor), Richard Tice (CLS Holdings) and Jonathan Seymour Williams (developer). Leave.EU's partners include Global Britain, whose business group includes Patrick Barbour (of Barbour Logic, who donated £500,000), Robin Birley (half-brother of Zac Goldsmith and a nightclub owner), Adam Fleming (billionaire chairman of asset company Fleming Family and Partners), Robert Lowe (transport), Hugh Osmond (Sun Capital Partners), David Stewart (Independent Mortgage Matters), Mark Stone (construction), Andrew Sturdy (SSL Insurance Brokers) and Richard Tice (again).[40]

Although it gave the smallest contribution, the Bruges Group was founded by former PM Thatcher, presided over by Norman Tebbit and Norman Lamont (vice president), chaired by anti-social security ex-Tory MP Barry Legg (formerly of Hillsdown Holdings food group), and directed by Tory politician and military historian Robert Oulds. It describes itself as 'a neoliberal think tank which researches and publishes against European federation and against British participation in a single European state'. The Group says it has 'spearhead[ed] the intellectual battle against European integration, EU federalism, centralisation and enlargement'. A former Chancellor, Lamont worked for the investment bank NM Rothschild and Sons, becoming director of Rothschild Asset Management. He is also director of the hedge fund RAB Capital, works for the Balli Group (a commodities trading house) and is an advisor to Rotch Property.[41]

WAGTV, part of the Leave camp, is run by Martin Durkin, who has produced documentaries such as: *Against Nature*, which criticised and allegedly misrepresented environmentalists; *Storm in a D-Cup*, which claimed that silicon breast implants may have medical benefits and that the dangers had been exaggerated; a pro-genetic modification film called *The Rise and Fall of GM*; and, perhaps most controversially, *The Great Global Warming Swindle*. Durkin also made *Britain's Trillion Pound Horror Story*, which blamed the national debt on high taxes and social security, and *Brexit: The Movie*.[42]

June 24: 'What a day!'

According to analysts at Preqin, although most hedge fund CEOs got the outcome wrong, 'no manager expected to see a negative impact', following the Brexit result. Private capital managers (of infrastructure, natural resources management, private equity, real estate and venture capital) were split, with a slight majority seeing Brexit as negative in the long-term.

Most private capital managers expect investments in the UK to decline in the short-term, but most hedge funds expect UK investment to increase.[43]

Eight months before Brexit, NexChange wrote that 'billionaire hedge funds are supporting the drive to take Britain out of Europe, and stand to benefit financially from such a move'. *Bloomberg* quotes Philippe Ferreira of Lyxor Asset Management: 'This [uncertainty] is typically an environment conducive for hedge funds who can trade the higher volatility and outperform traditional markets'. Although Reuters reported that the average hedge fund was down 0.18%, it also reported that computer-run hedge funds were up on average 0.71%. One day after the Brexit vote was revealed, the *Wall Street Journal* published an article titled, 'Some hedge funds clean up after Brexit vote'.[44]

Crispin Odey of Odey Asset Management gained 15%, 'paring half [the company's] losses for the year'. 'What a day[!]', he said. His Absolute Return Focus fund was up 6%. AQR Capital Management LLC's Systematic Macro fund gained 5.2%. Aspect Capital's Diversified Fund gained nearly 4%. Cantab Capital Partners Quantitative Fund gained 3%. Gold climbed 4.7% to $1,320 a troy ounce (a traditional weight) on the Comex NY Mercantile Exchange. George Soros, who famously bet against the pound in the early-1990s, making tens of millions of dollars, bought stocks and shares in Barrick Gold shortly before Brexit. Barrick Gold rose 5.8% as investors headed for safe markets. Steven Cohen's Point72 Asset Management has an internal memo from 24 June, stating: 'Following the UK referendum result, we re-emphasise our commitment to growing our London office as part of our international growth strategy'. This says a lot about the freedom that hedge funders and other financial service providers can enjoy after Brexit.[45]

Pro-remain David Harding of Winton Capital Management gained 3.1%, as bets were made against the British pound and the euro. Canadian Prem Watsa's insurance and investment firm, Fairfax Financial Holdings, was up 3.6%. 'They have massive derivative bets geared to pay off in a major way for this black-swannish situation', says David Havens of Imperial Capital. *Business Insider* reports that NuWave Matrix Fund was up 12%. Stanley Fink's ISAM Systematic Master fund gained 4%.[46]

Brexit: 'All business will benefit'

The financial shockwaves which brought the pound to a 30-year low after the announcement of Brexit were not only not-so-shocking for some, they were beneficial for others. A weaker pound helps British businesses export more products. Prior to Brexit, Barclays printed a report, stating: 'while a decision on Britain's membership ... may have important social, political and economic ramifications for the UK, it is unlikely to be a decisive factor for its capital markets – UK markets tend to dance more to the tune of factors born outside of the UK and even of Europe'.[47]

A JPMorgan report for fund managers states that investors won't do badly out of Brexit. JPMorgan predicts 'a rush to safe-haven assets', like the US dollar and Japanese yen, as well as European gilts and bonds (which are underwritten by taxpayers). The JPMorgan Equity Income Fund will 'benefit from this flight to quality at the very least on a relative basis'. The analysts also discuss how buyers bought up declining stock on the cheap ('downside capture') in equity markets, and note that regional banks and insurers 'should do well' compared with 'money center banks'. Other industries that will do well are financial services in 'utilities, telecoms, major oil, healthcare and staples stocks'.[48]

According to insurance providers AXA, 'far reaching reforms that might give a new life to the European project' are being considered in the wake of Brexit. The report says that while 'sterling and European equity markets [are] sharply down', so-called 'safe haven vehicles', such as the US dollar and Japanese yen, 'German Bunds, US Treasuries and Gilts, [are] sharply up'. This gives investors reasons to be cheerful, the analysts conclude.[49]

Some of Britain's wealthiest companies are: Shell, BP, HSBC, Glaxo, Vodafone, RBS, Barclays, HBOS, AstraZeneca, Anglo American, Lloyds, Tesco, British American Tobacco, Rio Tinto, Diageo and BT. Most of the companies had representatives sign a letter, which was co-signed by over a thousand other corporations, stating Britain's case for Remain. Despite the pro-EU rhetoric, few of these companies experienced losses as a result of Brexit. The details demonstrate how internationalized markets really are.

A weaker pound actually helps some exporters and as many of the companies trade in dollars, downturn in UK stocks didn't matter anyway. *Forbes* business magazine says: 'A Brexit might be advantageous to a number of UK exporters, as their goods will command more competitive prices overseas. Analysts at Credit Suisse noted that the positive impact of a falling pound could "more than offset the potential underlying business risks."' 'The direct impact [of Brexit] on us is very small', says Rio Tinto CEO, Jean-Sébastien Jacques. Rio's stock rose 1.3% following the Leave result.[50]

'[F]or every loser in these currency gyrations, there are winners', says *International Business Times*. '[C]ompanies that export from the UK to Europe have gained a 10% competitive advantage through a cheaper currency. In addition, companies that compete in global markets priced in dollars should also benefit from the pound's sharp drop against the dollar'. Winners include BAE and Rolls-Royce, credit rating agency Experian and pharmaceutical giants Glaxo and AstraZeneca, because 'much of their global earnings come from the key US pharmaceuticals market'.[51]

According to the *Wall Street Journal*, after a short plunge, Shell and BP's profits were up. '[M]any of the London-based companies' costs are billed in the plummeting pound, while their revenues are largely paid in dollars', says the WSJ, citing analysts with Tudor, Pickering, Holt & Co. 'The currency gyrations have also bolstered the dividend yield at BP to 7.6% and Shell to 7.5% "with no change at all in their abilities to fund the dividends", the Houston investment bank said'. Tudor, Pickering, Holt & Co. continues: 'Clearly there will be short term volatility but for those taking a long term view we see this as an attractive buying opportunity'.[52]

Business Insider reports: 'chief precious metals analyst James Steel and his team at HSBC say that the precious metal [gold] will take off after a Leave vote . . . when market turmoil will remain supreme'. The HSBC report itself says: 'The drive higher may be more pronounced if there were to be broader concerns about the future direction of the EU after the vote'. It is in the interest of some to keep the uncertainty going about Brexit. 'Gold could also benefit from the reluctance of investors to move into the GBP [sterling] or even the EUR

[euro]'. The analysts 'anticipate a sizeable safe haven bid in gold in this event'.[53]

24/7 *Wall Street* investments reports that as well as making a killing in gold, the Bank of England could prop up the banks. Again. 'HSBC has been such a poor performer for the past three years that it is already nearing its post-2008 financial crisis lows', say the analysts. 'A Brexit could easily bring it below those lows in a knee-jerk reaction, but then the Bank of England probably will rush to pump it with more liquidity in an attempt to calm markets'. They conclude that 'HSBC holds $2.6 trillion in assets, which makes it the most likely to receive central bank injections. This could slingshot the shares back up'.[54]

RBS is owned by the government, which bailed it out after the taxpayer forked out £45bn. Chief executive Ross McEwan says that Brexit didn't interfere with the Bank's diversification trend. 'We've got a plan that is working because we've restructured the business exactly as we said we would. We have a core business here that still makes quarter on quarter £1bn of pre-tax profits', thanks in part to the taxpayer. 'So it's a very solid business that we are concentrating on'. JPMorgan said of Lloyds, pre-Brexit: 'We view the elevated uncertainty ... as an opportunity to add to our top UK bank long-term pick Lloyds ... which also remains our highest conviction UK idea into second-quarter results'.[55]

The Drinks Business reports: 'Diageo's shares surged in the immediate aftermath of the vote to leave. From below £18 before the vote, at the time of writing they have jumped to almost £20 each, which marks a new high for the past 12 months'. The report says that '[a]t the time of writing it has lost about 10 cents against both the US dollar and the euro.

Less than 10% of Diageo's revenues come from the UK market, so a weaker pound benefits its top line profits'. *Bloomberg* reports similar profits for similar reasons for British American Tobacco. After Brexit, Vodafone experienced 'the strongest acceleration in growth for five quarters', says Polo Tang of UBS analytics. Despite UK stock plummeting, the company did well in Europe and in the so-called emerging markers. The *Independent* states: 'Chief executive officer Vittorio Colao is succeeding in reviving growth in European markets such as Germany and Italy, while relying on developing markets such as India, Turkey and Egypt for customer gains'.[56]

Brexit appears to be good for the pensions industry. BT reports that Standard Life Management Pension (worth £20 billion) increased 2.1%. Scottish Widows' Balanced fund (£8.1bn) rose 4.3%. In one of his last acts as Chancellor, George Osborne announced that corporation tax in the UK could go as low as 15%. '[A]ll businesses will benefit', says BT. Especially the big ones.[57]

Chapter 2

The Empire Strikes Back

Over the last decade, UK-EU trade and investment has declined while UK investment in non-EU countries has increased. British policymakers and business strategists complain that the EU is too inward-looking. Since the financial crisis, Europe's economic growth has slowed. When compared to the Commonwealth (Australia, Canada, India, New Zealand, etc.), EU sluggishness is all the more apparent. By concentrating political and legal attention on the EU, British policymakers and business planners say they are missing out on lucrative foreign markets. So-called developing markets have lower wages and production costs and higher profit potential than the EU.

'Projecting power globally'

As Britain's trade and investment with Europe declines, its foreign policy becomes more hawkish. Since 1998, Britain and America have escalated their illegal bombing of the third world in order to force non-compliant countries into what they call the 'rules-based system'. As Britain backs away from the political and economic European Union, it moves into the so-called developing world to 'exploit' resources, as the Ministry of Defence puts it.[1]

According to a British House of Commons Library report on Brexit, '[t]he share of UK exports going to the EU has declined in recent years. In 2002 the EU accounted for 55%

of UK exports ... In 2014 it accounted for 45% of UK goods and services exports (£230 billion) and 53% of UK imports (£289 billion)'. The UK government's review of competences on the Single Market – which assessed whether or not the UK should remain in the EU – shows how Britain's global foreign direct investment (FDI) has increased in recent years outside the EU, in line with its hawkish foreign policy: 'The UK is the world's second largest foreign investor, second only to the US, and has a stock of outward FDI of just over £1.1 trillion in 2011, a record high and having risen by around 75% since 2002'.[2]

PricewaterhouseCoopers (PwC) says that by 2011, the so-called developing economies contributed 10% of outward investment flows worldwide. Brazil, Russia, India and China (the BRICs) constituted 3.3% of total UK inward FDI stock by 2013. However, 'this share has tripled since 2001. India and China have been the main contributors', says PwC. 'The UK's key strengths in attracting inward investment include access to a flexible labour force', meaning high levels of (im)migration, comparatively low wages, long working hours, and comparatively low union standards. It also includes 'world class technology', most of which is paid for by the taxpayer through the pharmaceutical, biotech, military and university industries, 'and well developed financial markets', meaning highly deregulated capital and financial services industries. 'A major opportunity for the UK lies in attracting further investments from fast growing economies like Russia, Mexico, South Africa and the Middle East, as well as China and India', the report continues, going on to note that '[t]he UK could also exploit the potential of its world class universities in attracting more R&D'.

For British workers, this means competing against third world conditions.[3]

The British government's report on the Single Market states that a priority of the UK outside the EU should be 'opening up emerging markets, including an agreement with Korea that provisionally came into force in July 2011 and is worth £500m to UK exporters'. It says that outside the EU, Britain should 'conclude trade agreements with strategic economic partners such as Canada and India, and launch comprehensive packages of negotiations with the US and Japan'. Working with these alone would help 'tackle the remaining barriers to over half the world's trade'.[4]

The decline in EU–UK relations correlates with Britain's expansion into other regions of the world. Under Tony Blair, British foreign policy moved to the right, with seven overt wars waged in as many years: Iraq (1998), Serbia (1999), East Timor (1999), Sierra Leone (2000), Afghanistan (2001), Iraq (2003) and Congo (2003), not to mention a host of secret/ dirty wars and wars by proxy, including in Colombia, Somalia and Nepal. These wars were only waged in collaboration with European states within the context of NATO, and many of them were entirely independent of Europe.[5]

The *Strategic Defence Review* 1998, published during the Blair years, states: '[w]e depend on foreign countries for supplies of raw materials, above all oil', and that '[d]efence serves the aims of foreign and security policy'. The British establishment is 'resolute in standing up for our own interests... [T]here are opportunities to be exploited'. The Royal Air Force, like the Navy, exists as 'a coercive instrument to support political aims'. The same policy continues to the present.[6]

The Tory government's *National Security Strategy and Strategic Defence and Security Review* (the *Review*) 2015, states: '[e]conomic security goes hand-in-glove with national security'. Economic security means profits for big business: numerous government reports state that maintaining a 'flexible' (i.e., poor) workforce is essential for a 'dynamic' and 'competitive' economy. National security means security for unequally distributed profits. 'We have chosen to invest in projecting our power, influence and values', the *Review* continues. This involves 'expanding our economic relationship with growing powers such as India and China', and, judging from the lack of interest the *Review* expresses in the EU, a more distanced political relationship with Europe.[7]

'Our long-term security and prosperity also depend on a stable international system that reflects our core British values', the *Review* continues, including 'property rights', which includes intellectual property for drugs, hi-tech inventions and biotechnology. The British taxpayer will be compelled to '[i]nvest in ... globally deployable Armed Forces ... [to] project our power globally'. While distancing ourselves from the political and economic system in Europe, we are 'expanding our [military] relationships with France ... and Germany ... and with allies worldwide such as Japan'.[8]

It is interesting that as the British establishment states its intention to trade with and invest more in China, it also states its intention to work more closely with China's military and economic rival, Japan. The US is not only expanding its military bases and fighter technology in Japan as part of its Asia Pivot strategy to encircle China, it is also forcing Japan to back out of its constitutional 'pacifism clause', which it imposed on Japan after WWII in an effort to take over Japan's regional empire.[9]

The UK is actively 'promoting closer relationships across the Asia–Pacific region, including with Indonesia, Malaysia, Singapore and the Republic of Korea'. Each of those countries has been subjected to British imperial attack: Indonesia in the 1950s and especially 1960s, when Britain helped install the Suharto dictatorship, which killed a million or more people and annexed two countries; Singapore, an ex-colony; Malaysia, formerly Malaya, which Britain attacked in a war for rubber and tin in the 1950s, killing tens of thousands and using chemical weapons against civilians; and Korea, which Britain occupied with 100,000 troops in the 1950s.[10]

In addition to revamping its old East Asia Empire, the British establishment is 'building stronger relationships with growing powers, including China, India, Brazil and Mexico'. Citing the Commonwealth, EU, G7, G20, IMF, NATO, OECD, World Bank and World Trade Organization, the report states: 'We use our membership of these organisations as an instrument to amplify our nation's power and prosperity'. This is one of the few times the EU is mentioned in the Review.[11]

The Review concludes: 'While the US, Japan and Europe will remain global economic powers, they face a growing imperative to improve their economic dynamism and competitiveness if they are to stay at the cutting edge of the global economy – which our reform efforts with the EU are intended to help address'. As Britain's pressure on the EU to deregulate faced growing opposition within the EU, the UK increasingly looked to states that were not part of a Union (i.e., comparatively unprotected) to push the neoliberal agenda via bilateral trade and investment agreements (e.g., with Colombia), and foreign direct investment. In order to bully, blackmail, intimidate and generally use force and the threat of force against 'developing' countries and their leaders, to make sure they adopt deregulation and neoliberalism, '[w]e will recruit and train over 1,900 additional security and intelligence staff across the agencies', including MI5 and MI6 smoking out foreign spies and gaining as much information on the rest of the world as possible. As the *Guardian*'s revelations about police infiltration of left-wing, socialist groups implies, this could also mean a rapid expansion of the infiltration of peace, justice and anti-neoliberal groups.[12]

The coalition: 'Selling Britain to the world'

In its statement on *The Review of the Balances of Competences* (2012), Foreign Secretary William Hague's advisers state: 'In the face of a shift of economic power to the emerging markets, the EU needs to be more outward-looking, more dynamic and more competitive on the global stage'. As the EU wasn't going to do that, Britain would.[13]

In the general election 2010, the Tories failed to gain an overall majority. The Liberal Democrats betrayed their voters and came to power with the Tories under a coalition government (which consisted mainly of Tories). David Cameron became Britain's second unelected Prime Minister in a row: his Labour predecessor Gordon Brown was also not elected by the British public.[14]

In Cameron's address to the Lord Mayor's Banquet 2010, his speechwriters explained that Britain's objective was 'a more commercial foreign policy. This is not just about making Britain an attractive place to invest; it's about selling

Britain to the world too [sic]'. Cameron's speechwriters continued: 'Some people think it is somehow grubby to mix money and diplomacy. I say, when it is harder than ever for this country to earn a living, we need to mobilise all the resources we can'. Cameron's speechwriters concluded that '[t]oday we trade more with the Netherlands than with Brazil, Russia, India, China and Turkey combined. We are not making nearly enough of the opportunities out there. That's why one of the first visits I made as Prime Minister was to India'.[15]

The BBC reported that Cameron took 'seven cabinet ministers and a huge trade delegation' to India, including representatives from Standard Chartered, Balfour Beatty and the British Museum. Representatives from some 50 British companies accompanied Cameron. Subsequently, the two governments signed an agreement 'between BAE Systems, Rolls-Royce and India's leading aerospace company, Hindustan Aeronautics Limited (HAL), to supply 57 Hawk trainer aircraft to India'. The word 'trainer' is a standard propaganda term for fighter-jet. 'It follows a previous agreement to supply 66 Hawk aircraft to India', the BBC added. The Liberal Democrat Business Secretary, Vince Cable, 'announced the government will allow the export of British civilian nuclear technology to India for the first time. The Foreign Office and Ministry of Defence have previously been against such a move because India is not part of the Nuclear Non-Proliferation Treaty', which, like Israel and India's enemy, Pakistan, it refuses to sign. (Britain exports nuclear materials to Israel, however, including graphite.) Cameron said the deal was 'evidence of our new, commercial foreign policy in action'.[16]

Aside from pure profit, selling bombers to India also pushes Pakistan – India's neighbour and long-term political enemy – to the defensive right.

The UK's 'new, commercial foreign policy in action' involves bringing two countries closer to terminal nuclear war (see endnote for details). Commenting on the arms sales to India, the BBC quoted Cameron as saying that 'it was "unacceptable" for Pakistan to support any organisation involved in terrorism', referring to the government-linked Laskhar-e-Taiba, which claims responsibility for attacking India – and is indirectly supported by Britain (see endnote). But it is okay for Britain to supply Pakistan's enemy with nuclear technology. Delegates from Barclays, Vodafone, SAB Miller and the English Premier League also joined the tour. 'Cameron is expected to call on India to reduce trade barriers in banking, insurance, defence manufacturing and legal services'.[17]

Cameron also visited China in 2010 and was 'joined by four cabinet ministers and 43 business leaders'. The visit was a 'vitally important trade mission'. Cameron 'did not refer directly to jailed dissident and winner of the Nobel Peace Prize, Liu Xiaobo', the BBC reported. Rolls-Royce won a £750 million contract as a result of the visit. 'Pressure had been mounting on Mr Cameron to raise the issue of China's human rights record', the BBC continued. Cameron's speechwriters and PR people got him to say that, 'we shouldn't be lecturing or hectoring' the Chinese government about how they treat their citizens. Jailed Chinese artist Ai Weiwei said that by refusing to address the issue, Cameron 'was putting trade ahead of human rights'. Cameron's speechwriters explained: 'Our message is simple: Britain is now open for business, has a very business-friendly government, and wants to have a much, much stronger relationship with China'.[18]

The BBC should have not only raised the issue of China's human rights abuses, but Britain's *support* for China's abuses. China is the world's assembly plant, so it is not surprising that Britain has nearly ten per cent of its foreign GDP tied to China, and that human rights abuses are to be expected with companies seeking to maximize wealth. As two authors writing for the Royal Institute of International Affairs explained in 1997: 'With so much money at stake, the world is likely to be quite forgiving of China's indiscretions', such as the Tiananmen Square massacre of 1989, in which 1,000 people were killed by government forces.[19]

China's Minister of Commerce, Cheng Deming, informed the BBC, 'that China wanted to buy a lot more hi-tech equipment, but was prevented by prohibitions on the sale to China of items that could have a military purpose'. The historical record shows the opposite, as does the contemporary record, on which the BBC did not comment. As New Labour exited and the Tory-Liberal 'coalition' entered, the UK sold China a record £101.3 million-worth of military equipment in the second quarter of 2010 alone.[20]

Europe 'distorts Britain's trade patterns'

Open Europe is a think tank committed to '[r]egulat[ing] business less'. It has published several reports on Brexit, including one co-authored by Raoul Ruparel of the British Chamber of Commerce. The report says that post-Brexit, 'the UK would be able to enter free trade negotiations without the constraint of reservations that may be raised by other EU member states – particularly those with a more protectionist mind-set', such as France. The report then goes on to give several examples of EU constraints on UK investments in non-member states:

Britain wanted the EU to extend the trade concessions of the Generalised Scheme of Preferences with Pakistan. This was blocked by Portugal (one of the poorer EU states), which feared that cheap Pakistani textiles would undercut one of its main national industries. With regards to Singapore and its regulation and financial services integration, the UK considers 'financial services liberalisation [a]s key'. But for the other EU member states, 'protection of geographical indications (e.g. Champagne or Parmigiano Reggiano) is of greater importance'. The EU is seeking to protect its geographical indicators like those mentioned, against competition from East Asian alternatives.[21]

Britain wants to speed up the TTIP investment deal with the US, but France opposes it, largely due to America's unwillingness to include a chapter on financial services regulations. With Canada, the UK wants to speed up the investment deal – the Comprehensive Economic Trade Agreement – whereas France and Germany are opposed to the ISDS provisions. ISDSs allow governments to be sued by corporations for interfering with their profits by, for example, raising workers' rights and environmental standards.[22]

Another example of EU regulations hampering British investments is with Mercosur – the South American trading bloc. Mercosur was negotiating with Britain and the EU, but measures were blocked, especially via France's fears of South American agricultural imports undercutting French agriculture. 'It is hard to envisage the UK blocking deals based on concerns over GMO food, ISDS or textiles', says Open

Europe. As British investment shifted toward the BRICs (Brazil, Russia, India, China), it declined in Europe.[23]

Business Insider reports that in terms of performance, the British and German economies are far ahead of the Eurozone, with the UK having 'more in common with the economic recovery in the US'. Thanks to aggressive anti-social security policies, the British government successfully robbed many sick and disabled of their meagre benefits, forcing those who did not perish into work programmes, including zero-hour contracts. The recovery, says the Trades Union Congress, was also being driven in part by unprecedented long overtime for managers. This put 'official' UK unemployment at a low 5.5% (with social drop-outs like drug dependents and 'sofa surfing' youth not included). Official unemployment in the rest of the Eurozone is as follows (2015 data): Greece 25.6%, Spain 22.5%, France 10.2%, Italy 12.7% (11.1% average for Eurozone). In essence, Europe is slightly more socialistic than the UK, which is driven by neoliberal policies closer to the US model, hence the article's comparison of the UK's performance with the US. Citigroup calls this the 'plutonomy' model, where a tiny elite sector dominates economic policy and retains the 'fatter profit share', to quote them.[24]

In 1973, the European Economic Community (the EU's forerunner) accounted for 37% of global GDP. By 2013, it had shrunk to 23%. According to the IMF, the Commonwealth has greater purchasing power than the EU. Between 2004 and 2014, the percentage of EC staff from the UK shrunk from 10 to 6. A report by Business for Britain states that '[t]he British Chambers of Commerce has shown that the total cost of EU regulation is £7.6 billion ($12 billion) per year ... Since the Lisbon Treaty came into force in December

2009, it has cost British businesses £12.2 billion ($19.3 billion) (net) in extra regulation'. This was followed by a Reuters report stating that even though a majority of businesses wanted to Remain, a growing number wanted out.[25]

Open Europe concludes that Britain can only benefit in the wake of Brexit if it pursues deregulation. '[T]he path to prosperity outside the EU lies through: free trade and opening up to low cost competition, maintaining a relatively high immigration (albeit with a different mix of skills), and pushing through deregulation and economic reforms'. Free trade means pushing British goods on foreign countries and erecting barriers to protect the UK from dumping. Low cost competition means British businesses exploiting the abundant labour in foreign countries, leading to wage decline and joblessness at home. Maintaining high levels of immigration means exploiting low-, semi- and highly-skilled workers who learned their skills aboard and can be easily pushed out of Britain once their visas expire and their jobs have been done. This is exactly the opposite of what many of those who voted Leave wanted: 'There is no doubt that such an approach would disappoint a number of people on the "Leave" side', the report continues.[26]

'Opening up the UK economy to trade with the rest of the world – including the USA, India, China, Malaysia and Indonesia – would be essential to economic growth post-Brexit', says the Open Europe report. 'However, this would mean exposing UK firms and workers to new levels of competition from low-cost countries, which could be politically very sensitive'. Fortunately for the establishment, the Tory government has adopted a number of measures to cripple the Labour Party which, under Jeremy Corbyn, could potentially seek to reverse these policies (see note for details). It has also continued the expansion of the police-state, giving MI5 unprecedented spying powers under Home Secretary and now Prime Minister Theresa May, and it has continued New Labour's trend of militarizing the police so that angry, disaffected protestors and rioters face Tasers, teargas and rubber bullets in response to seeing their industries close, cost of living rise and jobs become less secure.[27]

'In order to be competitive outside the EU', Open Europe continues, 'Britain would need to maintain a liberal policy for labour migration' – a blessing for the racist, xenophobic far-right, like Britain First, the English Defence League and the UK Independence Party, which, in the case of the latter, has absorbed many of Labour's votes. 'This means EU membership and the trade deals with third countries the UK is a party to via EU membership, currently cover nearly 63% of Britain's global trade in 2014'.[28]

The government's report on the Single Market states that British corporations will find bilateral regulations easier than EU-level regulations, citing data that suggest Britain's regulatory mechanisms are 2.5 times more cost-effective than the EU's. The report notes '[t]he speed and scale at which globalisation is shifting wealth and power towards emerging economies'. The government's report on trade and investment says that '[t]he increase in businesses trading from countries with an abundance of labour and natural resources, especially emerging economies like China, Brazil, India and Russia, has presented a challenge to countries like the UK', which has a smaller, older, generally less impoverished population, and fewer national resources.[29]

'One of the justifications given to support a different

relationship with the EU is that UK businesses are making insufficient headway in to the rapidly growing markets in the emerging economies, especially Brazil, Russia, India and China because the UK's membership of the Single Market distorts the UK's trade pattern', says the report. 'Emerging economies have become increasingly important as sources and destinations of investment', the report continues, going on to note that '[p]roduction chains have become global, with the production of a good no longer occurring in one country alone'. Although the UK exports goods, the goods – as opposed to services – sector is small. The UK has never accepted EU jurisdiction over foreign direct investment. The Commission states that the EU has exclusive competence over all types of investment, including foreign indirect, based on article 207 of the Treaty on the Functioning of the European Union, which also gives the EU competence over liberalisation.[30]

May's cabinet

Two Atlanticist political advisers, writing for the right-wing pro-'free market' Heritage Foundation, said two years before Brexit that Britain should leave the EU in order to weaken the EU and promote more neoliberal globalization. They write that if Britain decides to leave the EU, as it did, 'it must treat the negotiation of agreements outside of the EU as a genuinely live option. To do that, the U.K. needs diplomats who are prepared to negotiate, as well as to make decisions, about which nations it will seek to negotiate with first'. In this section we document how the May cabinet is stacked with pro-'free market' internationalist hawks, war criminals and buffoons.[31]

In July 2016, former Home Secretary Theresa May succeeded David Cameron as Prime Minister. The appointment of May (without a general election) and her cabinet signals a further shift away from Europe to the third (or 'developing') world. George Kerevan (Member of Parliament for the Scottish National Party) asked May: 'Is she personally prepared to authorise a nuclear strike that could kill 100,000 innocent men, women and children?' May replied: 'Yes. The whole point of a deterrent is that our enemies need to know that we would be prepared to use it'. This is not only an interesting inversion of the word deterrent – that the Bomb will be used in order to deter it from being used – it also sends a signal to non-nuclear countries: that Britain has the means to attack them with conventional forces and be free from reprisals because any act of defence could be met with the ultimate weapon. The Falkland Islands is an example of this. In 2012, when Argentina started making diplomatic moves to compel Britain to decolonize the Islands, Britain sent a 'nuclear submarine' – armed or not, we don't really know – to intimidate Argentina's Kirchner government into withdrawing its diplomatic position.[32]

Two Royal Institute of International Affairs authors explain: 'The British do not have to flaunt their nuclear capability. Both friends and enemies know of its existence and behave accordingly'. Admiral Sir Raymond Lygo, a British Aerospace CEO, former Chief of Naval Staff and co-author of an Oxford Research Institute study, explains that nuclear weapons enable Britain to attack non-nuclear powers without fear of reprisal: 'Having a nuclear deterrent does give us the freedom to operate at lower levels of conventional military capability should we be required to do so politically'. The word 'deterrent' should therefore be replaced with 'enabler'. The MoD itself notes 'the capability to undertake nuclear action on a more limited scale in order to demonstrate our willingness to defend our vital interests to the utmost, and so to induce a political decision to halt aggression without inevitably triggering strategic nuclear exchanges'.[33]

May's cabinet also signals a more internationalist stance.

May studied geography at Oxford and, after leaving the Bank of England, worked as Senior Adviser on international affairs at the Association for Payment Clearing Services (APCS). APCS (now UK Payments Administration) facilitated the payment industry by supporting systems like the Bankers' Automated Clearing Services, Clearing House Automated System (CHAPS), the Cheque and Clearing Company, and other systems of the deregulated paper and digital currency sector which contribute to the boom-bust, stop-start economics of post-1970s' Britain. May then went on to work as MP for Maidenhead. Her first non-shadow ministerial job was Home Secretary under the Tory-Liberal 'coalition' government (which was about 80% Tory), where she deported 48,000 foreign students, telling policymakers to 'toughen up' on visa applications and rely more on UK students.[34]

Hammond:

Oxford graduate Philip Hammond was appointed Chancellor by May's advisors. A former consultant on Latin America at the World Bank, Hammond was appointed Defence Secretary in 2011 by Cameron's advisors. During his tenure, he informed Iranians, who were suffering US–EU sanctions on medicine: 'We can definitely make the pain much greater'. He went on to explain that the purpose of the sanctions was to impel the population of Iran to overthrow their government. Instead of being put on trial for war crimes under the Third Geneva Convention – sanctions being an act of war – and for crimes against humanity at the Hague, Hammond was then appointed Foreign Secretary by Cameron, where he oversaw secret wars in, and eventually the outright bombing, of Syria.[35]

Johnson:

Oxford graduate Boris Johnson was appointed Foreign Secretary by May's advisors, to the surprise and disgust of many. Johnson worked at the *Times*, *The Spectator* and as the *Telegraph*'s Brussels correspondent. Johnson is a well-known Eurosceptic. It sends a signal to the world that Britain is not only prepared to use apocalyptic violence to have its way (i.e., nukes), but that Britain considers its trade and investment partners vermin. This puts other countries and peoples at a psychological disadvantage.

Johnson said, perhaps ironically, that the Commonwealth supplies the Queen 'with regular cheering crowds of flag-waving piccaninnies' (an archaic, racist word for small black children). He said, in sarcasm to Tony Blair, that the Congolese 'will all break out in watermelon smiles to see the big white chief touch down'. On Uganda, Johnson wrote: 'The problem is not that we were once in charge, but that we are not in charge any more ... [T]he British planted coffee and cotton and tobacco, and they were broadly right ... If left to their own devices, the natives would rely on nothing but the instant carbohydrate gratification of the plantain'. 'We do not need to teach babies Mandarin', said Johnson, 'compared with the old British Empire and the new American imperium, Chinese cultural influence is virtually nil'. Johnson also referred to ping pong (a Chinese invention) as 'wiff-waff'. He wrote a poem alleging that Turkey's leader, Erdoğan, had copulated with a goat. At a meeting of the World Islamic Economic Forum, London, Johnson said that Malaysian women 'have got to [go to university] to find men to marry'. He also compared British party politics to 'Papua New Guinea-style orgies of cannibalism and chief-killing'. He described Russian President Putin as 'looking a bit like Dobby the House Elf', from the Harry Potter franchise. Johnson also outed journalist Dominic Lawson as an MI6 agent 'for a laugh' (to quote the media).[36]

Patel:
Priti Patel has been appointed Secretary of State for International Development. Patel is the daughter of a Gujarati–Ugandan refugee family, who were effectively ethnically cleansed as a result of Ugandan dictator Idi Amin's anti-Asian policies. (Amin, incidentally, used to work for the British as a thug in colonial Kenya and was then helped to power in Uganda by the British secret services.) Patel graduated from the University of Essex and joined the single issue Referendum Party, which pushed to leave Europe. Like others in May's internationalist cabinet, Patel is a noted Eurosceptic. After working for the Tories, she joined the Weber Shandwick PR company, lobbying for British American Tobacco to hide its abuse of Burmese workers, who were paid £15 a month, compared with Patel herself, who earned a £165-an-hour salary. After devising strategies to counter the UN's World

Health Organization report on tobacco, she worked for the alcohol firm, Diageo.[37]

Patel also contributed to a book, *Britannia Unchained*, which champions the neoliberal agenda, eliminating social security, ending workers' rights and making Britain supposedly more competitive with so-called developing countries. The book portrays Europe as a dead economic horse, in which there is no point continuing to flog. The authors – each of them rich Tory MPs – criticized Britain's 'diminished work ethic and a culture of excuses.... The dependency culture has grown dramatically', whinge the contributors, who of course don't refer to their own dependence on taxpayer revenues. The authors advocate reducing Britain's standards even further to force workers to compete with the poor of 'India or Brazil'. The authors are 'unembarrassed about [their] support for business, the profit motive and the individual drive of the wealth creator'. The book states: 'Once they enter the workplace, the British are among the worst idlers in the world ... Whereas Indian children aspire to be doctors or businessmen, the British are more interested in football and pop music'.[38]

Fox:

Liam Fox, Secretary of State for Trade, is the former Defence Secretary. Fox voted for the invasions of/retaining troops in Afghanistan, Iraq and for bombing Iraq in response to the rise of ISIL. He is an Atlanticist: a founding member of the Atlantic Bridge, an organization whose aim is to deepen British ties with the US. Fox backs NATO and is Eurosceptic. Seemingly unaware of his own hypocrisy, Fox has criticised abortion because the Bible says 'thou shall not kill, it doesn't say, thou shall not kill unless Parliament says it's OK'. Unless one is voting to kill Arabs.[39]

Fox graduated from the University of Glasgow and practised as a GP, during which time he made homophobic remarks: 'I'm actually quite liberal when it comes to sexual matters. I just don't want the gays flaunting it in front of me'. Claiming that he has matured since then, Fox voted against same-sex marriage in 2013 and, in 2016, announced that Britain would be trading with Virginia at a time when many are boycotting the state on account of its anti-transgender policies. Fox claimed over £20,000 from the taxpayer to mortgage a second home, which was revealed during the expenses scandal 2009. Fox repaid the money (but then appealed the decision). He also claimed £19,000 in phone expenses over a four year period. Fox later voted for welfare reform, but not to reform welfare for the rich, like MPs' expenses. Fox also accepted £50,000 from Jon Moulton of Better Capital, which went on to buy Gardner Aerospace, which supplies components for military and civilian aircraft.[40]

Fox has previously served as Under-secretary of State for the Foreign and Commonwealth Office, where he developed the Sri Lankan Development Trust allegedly to profit from infrastructural damage and rebuilding after the first phase of Sri Lanka's civil war, which Britain facilitated. Fox was accused of jeopardizing national security by granting his civilian friend, Adam Werritty, access to the Foreign Office and the Ministry of Defence. When Fox was Defence Secretary, MI6 secretly trained fighters in Libya to depose the Gaddafi regime. They did the same thing in Syria with the aim of deposing President Assad. These terrorists acted as provocateurs to justify foreign invasion of those countries. NATO illegally bombed Libya in 2011. At that time, terrorists linked to the UK were also operating in Iran in opposition to the government. In October 2011, Fox resigned for breaking the ministerial code over his relationship with Werritty.[41]

Chapter 3

Free Trade: The Americas

Many workers in Mexico and Brazil are brutalized by government-linked gangs and police. They constitute a captive market. Without safeguards, British workers will have to compete with labour in high-repression countries like Brazil and Mexico. Outside the framework of the European Union, British businesses will seek to draft bilateral trade deals. This includes the US and Canada on issues such as agriculture, energy and the privatization of services. This chapter documents the conditions in those countries.

Canada

'Free trade agreement' (FTA) is 'an obvious propaganda term' (Dr David Graeber). FTAs are not free, they have little to do with trade, and most of the affected publics do not agree to them. They are deals negotiated in secret by corporate lawyers and policymakers. They often include a number of protectionist measures, many of them hidden, which put the weaker of the two negotiating countries at a disadvantage. Such measures can include government subsidies to certain domestic businesses in country x, while country y is obliged to privatize its given industries.[1]

FTAs also allow for a number of hidden tariffs called non-tariff barriers to trade. These amount to hidden costs for country y. They also allow one country to maintain a surplus of trade over another. FTAs frequently allow multinational corporations to license their patented goods, such as medicines and technologies, often at the expense of domestic producers, who could have otherwise made those products cheaper and more efficiently.[2]

Nobel Laureate and former World Bank chief economist, Professor Joseph Stiglitz, writes: 'the intellectual property regimes designed inappropriately not only reduce access to medicines but, also, result in a lower economic efficiency and may even slow down the rhythm of innovations, with weakening effects, particularly serious in developing countries'. FTAs permit country x to open assembly factories in country y and then re-import or send the manufactured good(s) to country z. This is called 'foreign direct investment' and has as much to do with 'trade' as licensing.[3]

In 2009, at a time when British policymakers on the right were seriously considering backing out of Europe and weighing up the pros and cons of Remaining, the UK was strongly advising Europe to negotiate a 'free trade agreement' with Canada, calling, along with eastern European states, 'for the earliest possible entry into force or application of the Agreement' (leaked memo). The agreement didn't seem to matter much to the UK, because despite being prevented under EU rules from entering into a customs union with Canada (such as reducing and eliminating tariffs), UK imports of Canadian goods were three times higher than Germany's: Germany being the second biggest importer of Canadian products. Other European countries import from Canada about a tenth as much as the UK.[4]

The UK wanted a deal to further reduce barriers to trade, but it was also good for the City of London Corporation to push European countries into such an FTA. The reason being that if Canada and France, for instance, want to start expanding their financial services products, like derivatives, reinsurances, bonds, etc., they can do so in London, where regulation is far weaker than in Canada or France.[5]

The major problem with this arrangement, however, is that European countries are getting more regulated and more protectionist. This is partly due to a public backlash against economic globalization, which is still blamed (correctly) for the Financial Crisis of 2008, EU-wide austerity (2010–present), and consequences to jobs, social security and pensions. In the midst of this unrest, often suffering, European and Canadian free marketeers seized the opportunity to push through privatization schemes. They started negotiating the Comprehensive Economic and Trade Agreement (CETA), which explicitly seeks to privatize European and Canadian industry.[6]

The 1,598-page CETA document, finalized in September 2014, describes public subsidization as anti-competitive. It says that CETA should be implemented in accordance with World Trade Organization (WTO) rules. This means that if CETA is signed and ratified, Brexit might still tie Britain to the deal because Britain is party to the WTO, and certainly not likely to back out of the latter. Among generic legislation about reducing tariffs, CETA is so poorly worded and open to interpretation that there are provisions to allow European companies to access Canada's health system (including pharmaceutical licences), telecommunications, infrastructure and financial sector. And of course vice versa.[7]

Earlier, we noted how Canada and Britain (Britain being Europe's biggest CETA proponent) are 'plutonomy' countries, where the housing sector disproportionately props up the financial sector, the top 1% of earners has as much wealth as the bottom 90% and the rich stimulate recovery by spending on luxury services. CETA is part of a mechanism to transform European countries, however unrealistic this may be, into plutonomies. It is, in essence, a vital tool in the class war described a decade ago by multibillionaire hedge fund manager, Warren Buffett. Former Tory Trade Minister, Ed Fast, said that any Brexit deal would include a negotiated settlement on CETA.[8]

Brazil

The *Financial Times* reports that Brazil's Foreign Minister, José Serra, said the country is 'keen to supplement existing free trade talks between Mercosur and the EU with similar negotiations with the UK'. Britain 'imports relatively little from Brazil', said Serra, who will also try to convince the Mercosur bloc – Argentina, Paraguay, Uruguay and Venezuela – to back a trade and investment deal. (The FT reports that former left-leaning Presidents Lula and Rousseff, 'emphasised multilateral negotiations' over bilateral deals. But with the socialists out of the way, the right-wing President Temer 'is seeking to launch an aggressive new phase of trade negotiations'.[9]

Indicative of the new relationship, British farmers will compete with cheap, low-quality Brazilian beef and GMOs. *Bloomberg* reports that Brazil's big beef company Minerva SA, 'expects Britain to take a more flexible approach to meat shipments from [Brazil] ... which has faced EU restrictions'. Open Europe, whose report openly favours economic liberalization, says that in the event of a Brexit: 'liberalisation ... of the agricultural sector ... would mean creative destruction and would see a number of farms going out of business' in Britain.[10]

Until its socialist reforms, Brazil had an exemplary record on free trade:

In 1964, with help from the American CIA, the military took over in Brazil. This was immediately followed by inflows of US arms and military training. Thousands of left-wing students, journalists, political opponents and union organizers were rounded up and tortured with beatings, electric shocks and hangings for hours at a time in painful positions. The junta employed the British to devise more sophisticated forms of torture.[11]

Colonel Paulo Malhaes 'confessed to killing and mutilating his victims. He also expressed great admiration for psychological torture which, he felt, was more effective'. This was known as the English System. 'England was the best place to learn', he said. The British arrived in Brazil, teaching the military how to tap phones and keep records of activists, as well as collecting their corpses when the torture went too far. Ambassador David Hunt wrote to the Foreign Office stating that 'knowledge of this fact [i.e., torture] should be restricted'. A BBC report, which frames the story as Brazil's valiant efforts to fight the Soviets, says that 'a number of companies were involved'. Volkswagen's factory in Sao Bernardo do Campo, for instance, allegedly collaborated with the junta, allowing left-wing employees to be taken away and tortured.[12]

In the 1990s, British private firms, including karate specialists, were hired to train the Brazilian military and police. This included weapons training with knives and batons, as well as last-resort lethal force, chokes, and strangle holds.[13]

After the 1980s, Brazil started winning left-wing victories, with Lula's Workers' Party coming to power in 2003.

While cautioning against land ownership concentration and resource depletion, Oxfam nevertheless describes Brazil's massive poverty reduction over the last 15 to 20 years as a 'social/economic miracle'. Under the socialist government of President Lula and his Workers' Party, Brazil lifted tens of millions out of poverty, mainly with the *Bolsa Familia* programme, 'one of the largest welfare mechanisms in the world'.[14]

'[I]n its decade of implementation', says the World Bank, *Bolsa Familia* 'reduce[d] poverty by half in Brazil (from 9.7% to 4.3%) ... [P]arents receive a fixed monthly stipend ... in exchange for sending their children to school and complying with different health checkups'. Two economic historians note Brazil's reduction in financial pensions speculation, writing, 'the new commitment to universal pensions for rural workers has had a profound impact on reducing indigence and poverty among the older populations and especially those situated in the rural areas'.[15]

Lula's cabinet was rife with corruption and he himself was accused of taking money and granting favours to state-run corporations. The corruption is a side issue compared to how millions of Brazilians prospered under his brand of socialism. None of Brazil's achievements were reported in the bulk of Western media, which instead focused on the alleged corruption. Lula stood down in 2011 and was replaced by Dilma Rousseff, who had been tortured by the junta in the early-1970s when she was a Marxist guerrilla. Between 2015 and 2016, millions of protestors demonstrated against Rousseff, citing the Petrobas state-oil kickbacks scandal, for which no solid evidence has ever been presented. What most of the Western media failed to report is that the majority of anti-Rousseff protestors were 'rich and upper-middle class', according to Reuters, which also states: 'the working classes, even if disgruntled' by mass layoffs in 2015, 'have not wanted to associate ... with those who visibly turned out against Rousseff'.[16]

With Rousseff impeached, her vice president, Michel Temer, was also subject to a corruption investigation. Temer and oil executive Sérgio Machado conspired to lay the blame on Rousseff and exonerate themselves. Once Rousseff was impeached, Temer took over and proceeded to amend the constitution to limit public expenditure, privatize pensions, abolish state-oil funding for education and impose austerity. With Brazil swinging to the right and Britain announcing its plans to leave the EU because it is too regulated, the two countries started talking trade and investment.[17]

The Brazilian Chamber of Commerce in Great Britain complains that *Bolsa Familia* has 'a limited set of basic objectives: reducing infant mortality; ensuring children are better nourished and monitored by medical professionals; and reducing child labour'. These 'limited objectives' (keeping children alive and out of slavery) are hindering privatization. Brazil's devalued currency and rising interest rates have led to GTIS Partners, Brookfield Asset Management, Blackstone, GIC, Adia and other British firms buying up Brazilian land and property.[18]

In preparation for the World Cup 2014 and Olympic Games 2016, Brazil again hired British martial arts specialists to train groups, including the Command Operations Elite.[19]

'[P]opular uprisings jeopardized … long-planned hopes for capitalizing on the World Cup and 2016 Olympics', says the *Sports Business Journal*, with Coca-Cola, McDonald's, Visa and other big brands hoping to cash in on the advertising opportunity revising their marketing strategies. Fortunately, the police were there to silence the pesky protestors.[20]

Brazil has hosted both the World Cup 2014 and the Olympic Games 2016, during which a jaguar was paraded around and then shot by the Army. Both games saw a sharp escalation of police violence, with one in five homicides in Rio attributed to the police. In 2014, the Brazilian military occupied Rio de Janeiro's Maré favela complex for a year, shooting Vitor Santiago Borges, an innocent young man who lost part of his leg. Atila Roque of Amnesty Brazil, says: 'Killings by the police have been steadily increasing over the past few years in Rio. Many have been severely injured by rubber bullets, stun grenades and even firearms used by police forces during protests'. Britain supplies arms to Brazil. Roque concludes that 'the authorities still treat protesters like a "public enemy"'.[21]

Amnesty reports that when Brazil hosted the World Cup 2014, police shootings increased by 40%, killing 580 people. In the run-up to the Olympics, the toll in 2015 was 645. In the run-up to the favela clearances in 2012, ahead of the World Cup, Britain exported £176.9m in weaponry to Brazil, including assault rifles, combat shotguns, CS hand grenades, machine guns, small arms ammunition and weapon sights. In 2013, it leapt to £214m, and included anti-riot/ballistic shields, assault rifles, machines guns, silencers, drones and sight mounts.[22]

Mexico

After Brexit, Finance Minister Luis Videgaray said that Mexico has drafted a trade deal with the UK. Currently, 0.7% of Mexican exports go to Britain, equating to $4.3bn.[23]

Since Mexico accepted the Americanization of the peso in the 1980s and the North American Free Trade Agreement (NAFTA) in the 1990s, GPD has increased at an impressive rate. But the wealth is non-inclusive. Wages have stagnated as US businesses have shifted production and assembly away from domestic states to Mexico. Once assembled by cheap labour, the companies re-import their own goods to the US to sell domestically, nearly duty free. The US also invests in sweatshop factories known as *maquiladoras*.[24]

According to the OECD Better Life Index, Mexicans earn less than the OECD average and experience 'a considerable gap between the richest and poorest – the top 20% of the population [has] nearly fourteen times as much as the bottom 20%'. 68% of Mexicans are dissatisfied with the quality of their water. Mexico has a higher unemployment rate and lower voter turnout than the OECD average. 56% of women are unemployed in Mexico. 13% of OECD workers work long hours. In Mexico it is 28%. Of the 56% of employed women, 35% work very long hours. In other words, Mexico is a great country in which to do business.[25]

By 2014, UK-Mexico trade was $32bn. AstraZeneca, BAT, GlaxoSmithKline, HSBC and other big British companies operate there. Mexico is the second largest Latin American economy, following Brazil, and has a huge population 'of over 120 million', meaning many potential consumers and lots of unskilled, semi-skilled and highly-skilled cheap labour. 'Strengths of the Mexican market' for UK businesses include 'free trade access to the US market from Mexico under [NAFTA]'. The British government writes: 'NAFTA enables British companies to use Mexico as a low-cost manufacturing base with direct, duty free access to the United States'. Despite a drop in recent years, 2015 saw a near-21% increase in UK-Mexico trade, signalling the importance of the bilateral relationship. Mexico also has 'more free trade agreements than any other country – 11 agreements covering 44 countries with a potential market access of up to 60% of the world's [GDP]'.[26]

The 'challenges' include lack of protection for British products as Mexico has an 'open and competitive market'. Manufacturing, retail and real estate are the biggest sectors. 'Mexico is a manufacturing powerhouse', says the British government, accounting for over 60% of Latin American manufacturing exports. This is bad news for the British government's so-called Northern Powerhouse project, which supposedly seeks to reindustrialize the suffering north, because it will put British manufacturers in competition with Mexican manufacturers. 'Mexican consumers spend their money on', among other things, 'tobacco' and 'healthcare', says the government, as if the two are not related. This is good news for British American Tobacco.[27]

In construction, '[t]here are opportunities in ... alternative financing schemes such as Public Private Partnerships', where British companies get to plan and design Mexican infrastructure under tax-reduced foreign direct investments, where Mexican labourers toil on the projects, and the Mexican taxpayer pays for it. Opening up Mexico will also lead to more environmental devastation, following BP's catastrophic Gulf of Mexico wreck of 2010. 'After the sweeping energy reforms passed in December 2013, the Mexican oil and gas industry has opened up to private investment'. Much of the oil and gas is located in 'deepwater areas'. British companies have opportunities for consultancy, oil recovery and asset integrity management.[28]

Britain has what economists describe as a 'flexible labour market', meaning a high number of migrants, unpaid interns, zero-hours contracts, low pay and long hours (by OECD standards) and minimal unionization. This is great for business and is cited by free market economists as helping the economic recovery. Only a quarter of British workers are members of a union. Union membership is higher in the public sector (56% of the quarter), but with the massive privatization bonanza of the 1980s and public-private initiatives of the 1990s, the problem of higher public sector union membership was taken care of, to an extent. However, despite Tory efforts to change various laws relating to unions in an effort to weaken them further, Britain still cannot compete with Mexico for labour repression. Trade union density in Mexico was 15.8% in 1999. In 2014, it had declined to 13.5%.[29]

According to the US union, AFL-CIO, the 'single most serious threat' to unions in Mexico are the protection contracts between employers and employer-dominated unions, which are drafted and adopted without the knowledge of workers. Mexico's Labour Boards are controlled by the executive and are notoriously corrupt. The labour authorities routinely deny registration to legitimate unions. In ten years (2004–14), subcontracting has nearly doubled. This is a way for bosses to evade unions. In the mining and petroleum industries, health and safety problems are rife, with com-

panies refusing to conduct inspections, train employees sufficiently and compensate victims.[30]

Police and armed gangs regularly intimidate workers and
union members, on occasion killing them. Mexico also has a
chronic drug gang problem, with state-gang collaboration.
Amnesty International reports that in April 2016, Mexican
police and military officials were caught on video suffocating
a woman with a plastic bag. Amnesty says this is typical of an
institutionally brutal military-police establishment which
'routinely' tortures women – 'thousands' since the 1990s –
including with sexual violence and electrocution. This abuse
is part of the so-called war on drugs, where women are
interrogated and accused of being partners or wives of
wanted criminals. Sex workers are particular targets.[31]

Elsewhere, this author has documented how Western
special forces are facilitating a large part of the cocaine trade
in Colombia, which uses Mexico as a conduit. In 2010/11,
the American subsidiary of Britain's bank HSBC was found to
be laundering drug money for Mexican gangs. The facilitation
of drug-running in Colombia has dire effects in Mexico. Drug
gang violence was killing 10,000 Mexicans a year at one point
in the mid-2000s, with 60,000 dying in six years. Many of the
abuses occurred under President Felipe Calderón and his
security forces. '[S]ometimes acting in conjunction with
organized crime', state security forces 'disappeared' 250
individuals, says Human Rights Watch.[32]

The Toronto Star reports: 'Cartel violence has made Mexico
one of the most dangerous countries in the world. Now, the
criminal gangs have a new target – unions'. The report goes
on to note that, in 2006, methane gas leaked into the Pasta de
Conchos coal mine, causing an explosion that killed 65

people. The National Union of Mine and Metal Workers' leader Napoleon Gomez Urrutia and his family were threatened into exile in Canada. 'In states like Tamaulipas, the country's kidnapping capital, cartels ... expropriat[e] workers' dues ... as a new source of financing'. The Mexican Citizens' Council for Public Security and Criminal Justice wrote a 2014 report, documenting how '[c]riminal groups have significantly advanced their goal of controlling unions and their workforces'.[33]

British arms exports to Mexico have increased in recent years, leaping to £17m in 2014, including small arms ammunition.[34]

Britain is bombing Iraq (for the umpteenth time) and Syria, whilst also placing special forces in Libya, all under the pretext of fighting the so-called Islamic State. It is doing this, we are told, because ISIL drowns people, burns them alive and beheads them. Britain is not bombing its trading partner Mexico, where drug gangs, many of them connected with the government, boil people to death, burn them alive and behead them with chainsaws. There is one key difference: where ISIL crucifies its victims – as does Britain's ally, the Saudi monarchy – some Mexican gangs flay their victims alive.[35]

Los Zetas began as an enforcement branch of the Mexican Gulf Cartel. It consisted of 34 Mexican special forces soldiers and was tasked with protecting the leader, Osiel Cárdenas Guillén. Cárdenas Guillén became leader in 1999, hiring ex-Army Lt., Ruben 'el Chato' Salinas, who provided the gang with 30 army deserters. Los Zetas outgrew the Gulf Cartel and by 2003 was the most sophisticated paramilitary unit in the country.[36]

Several Mexican politicians are well connected to Los Zetas. The former governors of Tamaulipas (the 'disappearance capital'), Eugenio Hernandez Flores and Tomas Yarrington Ruvalcaba, are alleged by the US Department of Justice to have laundered money for Los Zetas. Yarrington is alleged to have been directly involved in drug trafficking. Heriberto Gonzalez Garza chaired an office of the Revolutionary Institutional Party. His wife, Cindy Apac, was arrested by the FBI for alleged money laundering. As head of PCR Consulting Services, Apac allegedly laundered money for Eugenio Hernandez Flores who is alleged to have secretly run the company. Another company, DUME, provided services for the Tamaulipas government, which was allegedly laundering money.[37]

The killings and beheadings, common for years, including the murder of women, have reached the level of political assassination. In 2012, 36-year-old ex-mayor María Santos Gorrostieta Salazar of the Party of the Democratic Revolution was murdered by drug gangs, following several assassination attempts. Aide Nava, a 42-year-old mayoral candidate for the same Party, was kidnapped and beheaded in 2015.[38]

The USA

To date, Britain and the USA have not signed any formal free trade agreements. The US was hoping to work out two such agreements – the Trade in Services Agreement (TISA) and the Transatlantic Trade and Investment Partnership (TTIP) – with Europe. As noted above and with the CETA case, the 'agreements' amount to whole-scale privatization of public assets and further capital deregulation. France and Germany were unhappy with America's refusal to include a chapter on financial services regulation in the TTIP agreement, and as we documented earlier, had made some efforts to constrain the actions of hedge funds and the like; much to the chagrin of the mega-rich.

Despite not having a deal negotiated, the USA is Britain's biggest export destination, accounting for $51bn of the UK's total annual exports ($473bn per year). Britain's biggest exports are cars, petroleum (refined and unrefined), gold, packaged medications and gas turbines. Indicative of how globalized the British economy is, its top *imports* are cars, petroleum (refined and unrefined), packaged medications and computers (total imports worth $663bn). After the US, Germany ($46.5bn), the Netherlands ($34.2bn), Switzerland ($33.6bn) and France ($27bn) are the UK's main export markets. Britain imports from Germany ($100bn), China ($62.7bn), the Netherlands ($50.7bn), the USA ($44.4bn) and France ($41.5bn).[39]

Where the UK excels, however, is exporting its dodgy financial products: the kind that helped cause the crash in 2007 and crisis in 2008. It has a global £61bn surplus (2013 figures). A whole quarter of foreign US corporate assets abroad ($5.1tn) are with the UK. British corporate assets in the US are $2.2tn. Britain has $487bn in foreign direct investment in the US. The US has $600bn of FDI in the UK. American firms in the UK employ 1.3 million persons, while one million Americans work for US-based British companies.[40]

Years before Brexit, Tory Member of the European Parliament Daniel Hannan said: 'Britain would have signed a bilateral free trade agreement with the United States decades ago', were it not for the EU. '[T]he barrier that is blocking a

U.S.–U.K. free trade area is the European Union', said two free marketeers (Gardiner and Bromund) a couple of years before Brexit. As Dr Giles Scott-Smith has documented, there is a long post-WWII history of various American agents of influence and organizations courting British politicians, particularly on the Labour left. This led to the rise of so-called New Labour. Some of these prominent Tories-in-red were one-time Labour leader Neil Kinnock, one-time Labour leader John Smith (who was on the steering committee of the secretive Bilderberg Group), and one-time New Labour leader and PM, Tony Blair.[41]

These individuals, and others from the left, had been wined and dined in the US, many given scholarships to study in America. This had the effect of hollowing Labour out from the inside and making sure that it was swayed to neoliberal, free market principles – quite in contrast to its own supporters, constituents and even against the wishes of many Tory voters.[42]

Dr Neil Gardiner is a British Atlanticist and Yale University graduate (home of the Skull and Bones secret society, of which three Presidents and one challenger have been members). Gardiner worked as foreign policy researcher for PM Thatcher, whom he helped author the book *Statecraft*. Gardiner is a regular personality on Sky and Fox. Ted R. Bromund is a professor of security studies at Johns Hopkins University. A fellow Yale graduate, he and Gardiner are members of the Margaret Thatcher Center for Freedom, which says its aims are to promote the values of Britain's deceased Prime Minister.[43]

Gardiner and Bromund authored a paper for the right-wing US Heritage Foundation, which represents the views of

American free marketeers. It says that the UK should leave the EU and negotiate an FTA 'with the United States'. The US, say the authors, 'should abandon its policy of supporting the EU at the expense of the sovereignty of its member nations'. Sovereignty means the sovereignty of financial institutions to evade regulation.[44]

The authors write that the Obama administration's strategy has been to use the UK as a 'Trojan Horse inside the EU' to push neoliberalism. Britain isn't strong enough and so the policy isn't working, they continue. 'The very fact that the U.S. is relying on the U.K. to strengthen its hand inside the EU also points out that neither the EU itself nor the U.S. sees the EU as aligning easily with U.S. interests'. A Britain unshackled from Europe would strengthen US-UK relations and weaken the EU in preparation for a regulatory assault by the US. '[T]he U.S. strategy of relying on the U.K. to carry its water in the EU will not work', they continue, citing the failure of the UK to block the appointment of the pro-federalist president, Jean-Claude Juncker.[45]

'[T]he EU is not an FTA as Americans conceive of it', the authors continue: 'especially in the realm of agriculture, it is a managed market that limits the ability of its members to trade freely with the outside world'. Corporate Europe Observatory notes that heavily subsidized US agribusiness is by far the largest lobby group for the US-EU TTIP deal. Current EU restrictions to US trade include barriers against hormone-treated beef, requirements for labelling genetically-modified foods and rules on endocrine-disrupting products like pesticides. Britain's regulations are more lax and the US is hoping to use Britain as a model to push its junk on the EU.[46]

Chapter 4

Free Trade: Asia

Britain is a minor export destination for the major Asian states: China, India and South Korea. Unhooked from the slow and shared 'free trade agreements' of the EU, Britain is free to export its financial products to Asia and in return boost imports of electronics (especially as Britain's economy relies more on services than it does on manufacturing), cars, clothing, toys, refined petrol and so forth. China has a captive labour force. India has a starving population. South Korea liberalized its economy in the late-1990s.

China

The great philosopher Homer Simpson once asked the Chinese: 'You guys are Commies? Then why am I seeing rudimentary free markets?'[1]

The reason being that between 1978 and 1993, China enacted a large number of 'reforms'. It privatized land, opened its markets to the West, and borrowed billions from the World Bank. GDP shot up and China eventually overtook Japan as the biggest Asian economy. The growth, as ever with 'free markets', was and remains highly uneven, with a huge gap between rich and poor. Although China has the second biggest economy in the world (next to the US), on a per capita basis the value of the Renminbi to the consumer (purchasing power parity) puts China 84th on the IMF's list of global incomes per capita. China ranks 90th in the UN's global Human Development Index. 119 million Chinese go without clean drinking water.[2]

China is experiencing the same sort of financial instability as its Western patrons: a housing bubble, currency devaluation, wage freezes, mass layoffs, strikes and the prospect of a pensions crisis. China exports over $2.3 trillion (tn) a year and imports over $1.5tn, meaning that Britain wants to open its market to China's goods. China's top exports are computers ($208bn), broadcasting equipment ($157bn), phones ($107bn), integrated circuits ($61.5bn) and office machine parts ($46.9bn). Its main imports are crude petroleum, circuits, iron ore, gold and cars. Most of China's exports go to the US ($432bn), Hong Kong ($258bn), Japan ($166bn), Germany ($101bn) and South Korea ($142bn). Its main imports also come from those countries.[3]

China is thus in the 'trading' position of importing Japanese computer parts and American iPhone technologies, assembling them in plants, and then exporting them to destination countries. China's economy would suffer if the US and Japan suddenly shifted assembly to eastern Europe or the Far East. The conditions for most of the workers in this assembly economy are horrendous. A lengthy report by the European Trade Union Institute points out that China's appalling working conditions have already set it in competition with eastern Europe, which is reducing its own labour standards. In particular, the world's leading assembler of electronics, Foxconn (based in Taiwan), is noted 'for the harsh working conditions in its mainland Chinese factories'. The report says that activists have highlighted Foxconn's alleged 'militarized disciplinary regime, unhealthy and unsafe working conditions, worker suicides, excessive and unpaid overtime, forced student labour and crammed factory dormitories'.[4]

According to the International Labour Organization and World Bank, China has a labour force of over 800 million persons. The Chinese have a range of skills, depending on education and training, including unskilled, semi-skilled and highly-skilled. This complex picture is made more complex by the fact that most of China's production is for export (of the kind of products noted above), not internal consumption. In addition, China hosts 269 million migrant workers.[5]

Until recent years, and as a result of strikes, things had improved. Layoffs and wage freezes were announced. America's AFL-CIO union states: 'China has been an attractive destination for global corporations' over the last ten years, 'due to its low wage rates and labor laws that disallow independent trade unions and limit the right to strike'. The report notes that China's industrial working class has gone on strike, forcing the government to negotiate. Despite implementing a number of anti-torture laws, '[t]orture and other cruel, inhuman or degrading treatment or punishment (other ill-treatment) have long been prevalent in all situations' in China, 'where authorities deprive individuals of their liberty', says Amnesty International. 'The Chinese government itself has acknowledged the extent of the problem'.[6]

Earlier, we quoted Cameron as saying that 'we shouldn't be lecturing or hectoring' the Chinese over their human rights abuses. The UK–China Joint Statement 2015 formalizes the agreement: it 'recognise[s] the importance each side attaches to its own political system, development path, core interests and major concerns'. China thus recognizes the hollowing out of British industry and the savage attack on social security. Britain, meanwhile, accepts and to a degree facilitates China's abuses, like those mentioned above. In Hong Kong, Britain trains the police force. Every year, Britain exports hundreds of millions of pounds sterling in military equipment to China.[7]

The UK is running a trade deficit with China (£18.7bn in exports compared to £38.3bn in imports). In trade-in-services, however, the UK has a surplus.[8]

In 2011, the UK–China Economic and Financial Dialogue, 'agreed to support the private sector to help London as an offshore RMB market', says the British Treasury. In 2013, the Industrial and Commercial Bank of China issued an RMB 2bn bond in London. A year later, the China Development Bank issued another RMB 2bn bond in London. This was described as a 'quasi-sovereign' bond; the first to be issued outside China. In 2015, the British government issued an RMB bond, 'the first non-Chinese issuance of sovereign RMB debt'.[9]

Trade and investment measures continued into 2015, with the Shanghai Stock Exchange and London Stock Exchange Group carrying out a feasibility study on stock connections. The UK and China also established a working group on mutual fund recognition. The People's Bank of China issued RMB 5bn in bank notes outside of China for the first time. China's central bank and the Bank of England increased their swap line – the amount that each country can purchase and repurchase – to RMB 350bn. The Agricultural Bank of China listed $1 billion of dual currency green bonds – supposedly for climate solutions – in London.[10]

In October 2015, Britain welcomed 'the largest contingent

of Chinese officials and business executives to arrive in London' in a decade (*Guardian*), where they announced the China-UK Joint Declaration on business, promising to make each side more 'competitive' through bilateral deals and talks, including the Annual PM's Meeting, Economic and Financial Dialogue, the High-Level People-to-People Dialogue and the Strategic Dialogue. This includes establishing a science and technology dialogue, the China-UK Innovation Cooperation Partnership. The statement says '[b]oth sides have a strong interest in cooperating on each others' major initiatives', including China's Belt and Road, and the UK's National Infrastructure Plan and Northern Powerhouse. The statement also mentions the China-EU Joint Investment Fund and Connectivity Platform between China and the European Investment Bank.[11]

In May 2016, Chancellor Osborne announced that China made available 'the first ever' RMB sovereign bond to international markets, 'underlining London's status as the leading western RMB hub'. This means that instead of trading toxic bonds with the US and EU as before, which largely contributed to the financial crisis, Britain can now trade toxic assets with China, anticipating an even worse future crisis, which will bring billions of profits to the culprits and misery to the tax-paying victims, as before. The statement patronizingly says that the UK is 'commit[ted] to being China's long-term partner on its journey of economic transformation and financial reform'. The 'journey' means internationalizing its financial sector and accepting trade and investment standards which have weakened the middle-class in Europe and America and polarized wealth. 'This landmark issuance is a significant step on that journey, signalling China's continued commitment to open its economy, liberalise its markets and internationalise its currency'.[12]

A month after Brexit, the government announced it was discussing further trade deals with China in an effort to shape the countries' first ever free trade agreement. The BBC reports that China would allow British banks to penetrate its financial sector '[i]n return for greater access to the UK for its manufactured products'. Chancellor Hammond says, 'as Britain leaves the [EU] and is not bound by the rules . . . perhaps it will be easier to do deals . . . in the future'. The BBC reports that '[c]are would have to be taken over . . . the possibility of China "dumping" cheap imports in the UK – for example steel'.[13]

Sheffield City Council has already taken great care. Sheffield in the UK is a city famed for its steel. The neoliberal programmes of the 1980s caused a major decline in the British steel industry. The University of Sheffield reports that the City Council made a £1bn deal with Sichuan Gudong Construction, lasting 60 years. This is supposed to 'boost the future economy of the UK's Northern Powerhouse', says Professor Sir Keith Burnett.[14]

India

India is the seventh largest economy in the world, behind the UK and France. As usual, GDP does not equate to per capita wealth. In a population of over 1 billion (bn), a quarter lives in abject poverty and approximately 200 million Indian children are starving at any one time. According to the World Bank mortality index, 38 infants in every 1,000 die before their fifth birthday. India ranks 130th in the UN's Human Development Index, behind Tajikistan and Iraq.[15]

In 2014, India's exports amounted to $292bn and its

imports $421bn. Its main imports come from China ($52.5bn), Saudi Arabia ($30bn), the United Arab Emirates ($24.4bn), Switzerland ($21.3bn) and the USA ($18.2bn). Britain is seeking to export more to India. India's main exports are refined petroleum ($53.9bn), packaged medicaments ($12.1bn), jewellery ($11.8bn), rice ($7.75bn) and cars ($5.82bn). The main exports go to the USA ($35.9bn), the UAE ($29.6bn), China ($13.9bn), Saudi Arabia ($13bn) and the UK ($10.6bn).[16]

India's main imports are crude petroleum ($122bn), gold ($31.1bn), petroleum gas ($17.7bn), diamonds ($17.5bn), and coal briquettes ($15.4bn). As numerous rights groups have documented much of the diamond cutting, jewellery-making and coal refining industries are based on modern slavery, including bonded labour (where one works to pay off a debt incurred by relatives), child labour and exploitation in the racist caste system, where Dalits (usually darker skinned Indians) are servants.[17]

India's experience of genocidal colonialism led to the government closing the post-independence economy. Technology, location, pricing and state-control over capital goods were closely coordinated. Trade was restricted by licensing and foreign exchanges were carefully managed. India largely ignored the US-led General Agreement on Tariffs and Trade (GATT), which was established in the late-1940s and designed to coordinate tariff reductions. Part of India's postcolonial tragedy was its so-called Hindu growth rate, where the 1960s' population grew at the same rate as GDP, creating a zero net impact on per capita wealth. By the 1980s, this was a negative, meaning that more people starved.[18]

India's constitution provides for semi-autonomous control over land and resources with power centred on landlords. In the 1960s, Maoists from the village of Naxalbari, West Bengal, formed the Communist Party of India (Naxalites) after its predecessor split. Their professed aim was land redistribution. The group had some support in poverty-stricken southern and eastern areas. In 1969, the Army planned for a counterinsurgency operation, Steeplechase, against the Naxalites. The latter threatened to assassinate class enemies, including businesspeople, landlords, lecturers and police. Steeplechase began two years later and ended in the killing of hundreds of Naxalites and the arrest of 20,000 suspects. As India began privatizing land and exploiting natural resources for domestic 'development' and export, impacted communities began supporting the Naxalite cause.[19]

Throughout the 1980s, prominent Indian intellectuals and lawmakers 'advocated privatization, state downsizing and the unleashing of market forces', write legal experts Shaffer et al. As part of what they call the 'new model', the state started propping up the finances sector, as well as pushing exports and lowering barriers to imports. India's internal changes resulted from external factors, the authors continue. US and British lawyers were drafted to help decentralize state controls over regional finance and investment. This amounts to what the authors call 'globalized localisms'.[20]

The Gulf War oil shock created a crisis for India's petroleum-dependent economy. The government borrowed $2.3bn from the IMF and exported gold to its old imperial master. The Rao government enacted a series of IMF 'adjustments', which included internationalizing India's economy. A report by the Confederation of Indian Industry notes than when the GATT transformed into the World Trade Organization (WTO), industrial planners were largely excluded from the negotiations. Under WTO rules, numerous cases were brought against India (compared to just three in its entire history at the GATT), most of them by the EU and the USA, whose businesses wanted India to take advice from foreign lawyers on how best to liberalize the internal market. This approach was led by the UN's Conference on Trade and Development (UNCTAD) and Britain's foreign privatization wing, the Department for International Development (which the British government portrays as some kind of charity).[21]

After 9/11, anti-Muslim sentiment gave rise to the right-wing Hindu nationalist party, the BJP, which came to power in 2014. Under India's counterterrorism laws, peaceful dissenters are detained and frequently tortured by the police, who regularly practice rape: something not mentioned by Western media, which suddenly became concerned with the rape of Indian women by gangs of men a few years ago.[22]

As part of Operation Green Hunt 2009, the Indian Army attacked Naxalite strongholds in regions marked for mining, damming and other pro-business developments, killing civilians in the process. Learning from its British masters, the Indian government continues to use vague laws, such as sedition and defamation to silence dissent, according to a 2016 Human Rights Watch report. Recently, Britain and India expanded their military training programmes, including operations on Salisbury Plain, UK, where Indian and British soldiers pretended to be 'insurgents' vs. members of the Indian Army.[23]

Britain's arms exports also continue to flow to India, with

£95.6m-worth of military equipment exported in 2014, including ammunition, guns, and components for all manner of weapons.[24]

The failure of the EU to settle a trade deal with India has prompted lawmakers to seek 'a new trade agreement' with post-Brexit Britain, says the FT. Ignoring the BJP's far-right tendencies and neo-Nazi connections, the UK will be looking to negotiate with the Party: 'If an FTA negotiating unit is 25 constituent countries with their own pluses and minuses', says BJP affiliate, Swapan Dasgupta, referring to the EU, 'you are not going to get to some sort of common ground ... But there is a far greater chance of it with the UK'. B.K. Goenka, chairman of the billion-dollar textile and pipe company, the Welspun Group, says that Brexit will be 'a win-win situation', with tariffs eliminated.[25]

Others caution that a weakened pound will harm India's UK companies, notably Tata Steel and Tata Motors. Akshay Chudasama, who manages the Shardul Amarchand Mangaldas law firm, says that India uses Britain as a base from which to trade with Europe, including IT and pharmaceuticals. New barriers to EU trade will hurt India's European trade. Others, however, like R. Chandrasekhar of India's IT industry association, Nasscom, says the EU is overregulated with respect to security policies and personal data. 'To our understanding ... the UK is not aligned to that mode of thinking'.[26] This will benefit software and data companies.

Presently, Britain's main exports to India are non-ferrous metals (primarily silver), gems and jewels, power generating equipment, ores and scrap metals, electrical appliances and professional apparatus (e.g., scientific equipment). After Mauritius and Singapore, the UK is India's third largest investor, accounting for 9% of the country's foreign direct investment. The UK is looking forward to India's domestic investments in 'large scale manufacturing zones', where British goods can be assembled cheaply and sold domestically or internationally. As the fourth largest energy consumer, India will likely expand its business with the BG Group, BP and Shell.[27]

India is great for doing business, says the UK's Department for International Trade, partly because 'it has removed the majority of its trade barriers to improve the business environment' and partly because of its 'availability of skilled, low cost workforce'; meaning widespread poverty and weak per capita buying power. The World Bank ranks India 130 out of 164 countries for per capita income value (purchasing power parity). India has already succeeded in 'opening the economy to foreign businesses and allowing overseas investment in multiple sectors'. The report goes on to note that India has 'huge potential ... [in] life sciences, manufacturing, energy and infrastructure'.[28]

South Korea

Far higher than China and India, South Korea is 17th on the UN Human Development Index. It is the 11th largest world economy. South Korea has a population of 50 million. About a quarter of the population lives in poverty, except the older generation. About 50% of elderly South Koreans live in poverty. Of the OECD countries, South Korea and the USA have the highest levels of wage inequality. Korea is the world's 5th largest exporter ($583bn per annum, importing $508bn). Its main exports are integrated circuits ($59.5bn), refined petroleum ($46.9bn), cars ($44.1bn), ships

($23.7bn) and LCDs ($21.4bn). Its main imports are crude petrol ($88.1bn), gas ($35bn), integrated circuits ($29.8bn), refined petrol ($27.2bn) and coal briquettes ($10.7bn). South Korea's export destinations are China ($142bn), the US ($70.1bn), Japan ($32.2bn), Hong Kong ($24.5bn) and Singapore ($24.3bn). It imports from China, Japan, the US, Saudi Arabia and Qatar.[29]

Why did South Korea, having been decimated with war, do much better than China and India? Hart-Landsberg and Burkett describe South Korea as an 'ideological battleground' between statism and 'free markets'.[30]

After Britain and America decimated Korea in the 1950s' war, its GDP was 40% below India's crushed economy. 40% of the population suffered absolute poverty. By 1990, the country had become the 12th largest trading nation. In the 1960s, South Korea accepted loans from the USA, the World Bank (which means the USA) and Japan (which means the USA). By 1982, South Korea's external debt was $37bn. Yet the money was spent on modernization and social protection. South Korea's rapid GDP growth is described as a three-decades long 'miracle'. Kwan S. Kim writes that unlike China's 'communist' fascism and India's democratic 'capitalism', the 'miracle' included 'relatively equitable income distribution'.[31]

Under the dictatorship of Park Chunghee, which the US backed for a while as a bulwark against the Soviets, the miracle involved industrialization away from agrarianism, with 90% of steel for instance used for domestic purposes. Real wages rose 370% from 1967 to 1978, 'in response to increasingly militant Korean labor unions' demands', writes Kwan. Despite the gains, Koreans worked over 50 hours a week, creating a disparity in wages-to-work hours. After Park's assassination in 1979, South Korea sought to balance its debts, inflation and crop failure by opening markets internationally, while retaining state controls over welfare. In the 1980s, Korea started exporting colour TVs, digital watches, microwave ovens and stereos to Europe, Japan and the USA. Through the central Bank of Korea, the government issued credit (policy loans) to various industries.[32]

Korea's hi-tech explosion was due in large measure to foreign direct investment, in which just under half of the given product to be assembled could be owned by foreign countries (mainly the US). Part of Korea's income inequality, which had been growing since the 1960s, was the over-investment in monopolistic companies, which gained virtual control over the direction of the economy.[33]

In the 1980s, Japan blocked some exports because its own producers and retailers were losing out to Korea's. Strikes broke out in 1987 in opposition to the country's long working hours and repressive labour conditions. The revaluation of Korea's currency, provoked by the US (a main creditor) resulted in a trade deficit. Japan's subsequent investments in Indonesia, Malaysia and Thailand also reduced Korea's regional status. In the mid-1990s, Korea began deregulating. As big Korean firms went bust, foreign investors started selling off Korea's bonds.[34]

South Korea's boom ended in 1997. Many economists cite South Korea's economic liberalization, deregulation and the abandonment of state planning and investment coordination. Into the 2000s, numerous US banks had bought up numerous Korean businesses. The EU–South Korea Free Trade

Agreement is 'the EU's first trade deal with an Asian country', says the EC, indicating its comparative inward-looking nature. The EU is South Korea's third largest export market. It is the EU's ninth largest export market, counted as a single bloc. The EU's imports are mainly machines, plastics, and transport equipment. South Korea also signed trade deals with the US and China.[35]

'South Korea's trade deal with the EU is ... the only one in East Asia', says the Wall Street Journal. British industry and retail could benefit £500m per annum from such a deal. Investors include BP, Shell, Diageo, HSBC and Prudential. As noted, many of those firms have benefited from Brexit. However, these same corporations (and others, including AstraZeneca) are mentioned years before Brexit. This indicates their desire for a bilateral UK-South Korea FTA.[36]

Over the last decade, 'South Korean companies have taken advantage of the United Kingdom's pro-investment climate', says First magazine's business analysis. In Chapter 2, we document how the Tory–Liberal coalition government initiated a review of the EU's competences and weighed the pros and cons of Britain's membership. As this was being planned, Foreign Secretary William Hague said that the UK had already set an export target of £1 trillion per annum to Korea by 2020. Britain and Korea will 'deepen ... commercial ties in everything from energy and high technology to education and financial services'. Rather than relying on the domestic talent of the millions of unemployed and semi-employed Britons of the present and future, the government will 'attract South Korean investment to British shores'. Hague said that the EU–Korean FTA retains some barriers, which President Park and

PM Cameron were looking to overcome via the UK–South Korea Joint Economic and Trade Committee.[37]

The UK Trade and Investment Office calls South Korea a 'high growth market', boasting 'opportunities' for the aerospace, creative and ICT industries. 'Creative industries' include the video gaming culture, which is so addictive that South Korea has set up video game addiction rehabilitation clinics, sparked by the famous case of the three-month old, Kim Sa-rang, who died of starvation as a result of parental gaming addiction. The 'high growth market' is driven in part by what Reuters calls a 'decade-long stagnation in wage growth'. It also provides a market for privatization. Had Britain stayed in the EU, says *First* market analysis, it would have acted as the EU's asset managers over acquisitions of South Korea's Investment Corporation and Pension Service. Thanks to the 'disposable income' of the middle-classes, there are '[m]ajor opportunities' to sell Koreans food, drink and cigarettes. The South Korean National Pension Service has invested $1bn in UK infrastructure.[38]

After Brexit, South Korea signalled its desire to sign an FTA with the UK. 'The sooner Britain can renegotiate deals with major partners outside Europe, the likelier EU leaders will be able to do the same', says the *Wall Street Journal*. The EU will do this, 'rather than try to punish Brits for choosing divorce', the WSJ continues. 'The most important partner in this regard is the U.S., which should signal immediately that President Obama won't follow through on his threat to send Britain to the "back of the queue" on trade'.[39]

Conclusion

'Finishing Thatcher's revolution'

Perhaps the best evidence for the truth about Brexit is Nigel Lawson's article in the *Financial Times* entitled, 'Brexit gives us the chance to finish the Thatcher revolution'.[1]

Born to wealthy parents working in the financial sector, Lawson is a Eurosceptic Tory. He had a career in money, working as a journalist for the *Financial Times* and City editor of the *Sunday Telegraph*. Lawson was appointed Financial Secretary to the Treasury in 1979 and became Chancellor of the Exchequer in 1983, having served as Energy Secretary. As Energy Secretary, and working closely with the Department of Trade and Industry, he oversaw the privatization of British Airways, British Gas and British Telecom. He is mostly remembered for presiding over the so-called Big Bang deregulation of 1986.[2]

After the Brexit result, Lawson wrote of his 'thoroughgoing programme of supply side reform' in the 1980s, 'of which judicious deregulation was a critically important part. But it was only indigenous UK regulation that we could repeal or reform', he continues. 'And increasingly we are bound by a growing corpus of EU regulation which, so long as we remain in the bloc, we cannot touch'. Lawson goes on to say that 'Brexit gives us the opportunity to address this; to make the UK the most dynamic and freest country in the whole of Europe: in a word, to finish the job that Margaret Thatcher started'. In conclusion, Lawson says: 'deregulation, something that cannot be captured in any theoretical economic model but which we demonstrated in the 1980s ... offers the prospect of the greatest economic gain'. That statement should be qualified with a reminder that the richest gain the most and the poorest lose out or stagnate. 'And this is entirely in our own hands, and not a matter of negotiations with others. That is what we need to be focused on now'.[3]

In this book we have highlighted the genuine grievances of working and unemployed persons who saw their livelihoods and prospects decline and who ultimately voted for Brexit. We have also noted the propensity towards xenophobia. England is where pro-Leave sentiment was strongest, particularly in the deindustrialized north. Instead of educating working and unemployed English people about the common enemy of neoliberalism, the tabloids and television media have given people the impression that migrants are to blame for job insecurity and a general decline in living standards. In addition, the skewed demographic character of the UK gave older people greater voting power. The polls show that older people were more inclined to vote Leave.[4]

In Chapter 1, we demonstrated that these concerns were hijacked by an old establishment of right-wing internationalists, bolstered by the new money of hedge fund CEOs, who share an interest in investing more in the Commonwealth countries (including Australia) than in Europe. Britain is not strong enough to influence Europe, but, with the USA, it is strong enough to influence many third-world Commonwealth countries. Britain also seeks to corner the growing financial services markets of Asia. Membership of the EU is preventing this. This book has documented exactly who these people are and given information about their political views and financial backgrounds. Chapter 2 demonstrated that Theresa May's cabinet is full of right-wing internationalists. This is not a coincidence, but a continuation of a policy to distance the UK from Europe in many ways. It argued that this policy, coupled with renewed dedication to global militarism, can only be to the detriment of poor countries. Before he stepped down as Prime Minister, Cameron announced plans to spend an extra £12bn on Britain's five-year military budget, worth £178bn. This includes buying 138 pieces of hardware, such as 24 Lockheed Martin F-35 Lightning II jets and a new generation of surveillance drones. Part of the plan is to cut jobs while buying more semi-autonomous hardware, including eight warships made by BAE, plus nine Boeing aircraft. '[T]hese investments are an act of clear-eyed self-interest to ensure our future prosperity and security', said Cameron. Interestingly, some of the aircraft are submarine hunters designed, supposedly, to protect Britain's nuclear-armed submarines. The deal 'follows an intense lobbying campaign by Boeing's rivals including Airbus Group, Finmeccanica and Lockheed Martin', says Reuters. More importantly, Britain's expansion of nuclear arms enables the UK to attack third-world countries and remain immune from attack, as experts cited in Chapter 2 reiterate.[5]

Chapter 3 examined Britain's role in the Americas, particularly in the relation to Canada's environment, Brazil's agricultural products and Mexico's factories. Consider the influence of British energy companies on Canada's environment. The European Union planned to categorize oil derived from Canada's tar sands and used in transport as highly polluting. This proposed regulation would harm oil companies investing in tar sands because transportation companies would be more reluctant to use tar sand-derived oil. More generally, extra regulation would have a chilling effect, said BP in confidential memos obtained by the Co-operative and Greenpeace UK.[6]

The EU–Canada CETA deal, discussed in Chapter 3, has the potential to make investing in Canada's tar sand oil projects even easier. In 2011, it was revealed that the Tory government, under the lobbies of BP and Shell, had given advice to companies and to Canada's Harper government on how to avoid or minimize European environmental penalties. Britain's Tory–Liberal coalition led the charge against the aforementioned tar sands regulation. Pressure from council tax-paying constituents has made local councils more responsive to environmental and human rights concerns. The Tory government, however, is so committed to profit-at-all-cost that in 2015, new 'guidelines' were announced by the central government in Whitehall advising local councils from divesting from certain countries (including Israel) and from certain businesses (including energy companies). The central government is blackmailing local councils, threatening penalization over divestments.[7]

Many local councils invest in all manner of stocks and shares, including oil and gas, particularly through their pension funds. Concerns have been raised by economists that these can amount to bad investments, given the fragility of the present fossil fuels market. More genuinely, environmental activists have pointed out the amorality of using public money to foster pollution and climate change. The group Go Fossil Free has compiled a dataset of every council across the

UK and where it invests in fossil fuels. It finds that £14bn of taxpayer money is currently invested in fossil fuel companies, including BP and Shell, which invest in Canadian tar sands.[8]

Chapter 4 of this book is the concluding chapter. It argues that China became a global power after adopting 'free-market' principles at the expense of its population, which faces mass layoffs, a housing bubble, high levels of repression and regular workers' strikes. In contrast, South Korea became a leading economic player by violating the neoliberal project, at least until the 1980s/1990s. South Korea's recent financial deregulation is attractive to London-based market players.

Britain is likely to increase its use of Indian labour. 'We will continue to welcome those who can fill gaps in the labour market which cannot be filled by UK residents', said James David Bevan in 2012. Bevan was High Commissioner of the United Kingdom to India. '[W]e have made special arrangements for Indians coming to the UK under intra-company transfers (where a company based in India wishes to send a staff member to work for the company in the UK). We have deliberately not set a limit on the number of Indians who can come to the UK by this route', Bevan continues. However, it works both ways. Over the last decade, British businesses, including small ones, have out-sourced their work to India, Pakistan and the Philippines. An analysis by Freelancer concludes that in 2015, there was a 20% increase in British outsourcing to China. Most outsourcing is in the IT and telecoms sectors. '[G]etting work done more cheaply' is one of the two reasons cited, according to *This is Money*; the other being a lack of domestic skills: skills which could be invested in the hundreds of thousands of disaffected youths who sink into isolation and despair.[9]

What can we do?

In conclusion, it will be difficult to force a government U-turn on Brexit. Theresa May has famously said, 'Brexit means Brexit'. We can question the government's rhetorical sincerity, but it becomes quite serious when the government announces its intention to use the Royal Prerogative to bypass Parliament, which otherwise has the potential to overturn the decision to Leave. Firstly, Remaining may not even be desirable, as many Britons want a Brexit. Forcing Remain would fly in the face of majoritarian democracy. Secondly, it raises the bigger question: What are we leaving? As this book has tried to address, on many important issues Brussels had no jurisdiction over the UK anyway.[10]

Rather, it may be a more sensible approach to focus on the key issue that unites everybody: neoliberalism. Do we want to continue to live in a world of conscious 'class warfare', as described by multibillionaire Warren Buffett, or do we want to push for a more equitable distribution of wealth? Do we want to live in a deregulated economy, which even some of those championing deregulation admit causes financial crises? Or do we want to at least live in a regulated Keynesian economy, as a first step towards something even more equitable, where wealth reaches the bottom quarter? One of the major challenges is to recognize people's anger and acknowledge that they have genuine grievances. The next challenge is to demonstrate to them that their frustrations are targeted at the weak (migrants etc.), when they should be targeted at the strong (e.g., free-marketeers).[11]

By building community associations and campaigning on specific issues, including economic regulation and industrial and educational investment, we can set aside the dialectical in-out distraction of Brexit and focus on putting an end to the dangerous neoliberal project.

Notes

Preface

1. Economists Sam Brazys and Niamh Hardiman include Italy in the PIIGS acronym, as do others. Writing specifically about Ireland, they conclude that 'the term had a clear negative effect on the country's market treatment, indicating that acronyms can act as signals that guide and shape market perceptions': in this case, the perception that Western Europe's poorer countries can be treated with contempt. They conclude: 'When economic journalists treat these countries as a bloc in their commentary, the effect is that they are treated as a bloc by investment managers'. See Brazys and Hardiman, 'The 'PIIGS' acronym had a clear negative impact on the response of financial markets to the "PIIGS countries" during the crisis', European Politics and Policy, London School of Economics, 12 December 2014, http://blogs.lse.ac.uk/europpblog/2014/12/12/the-piigs-acronym-had-a-clear-negative-impact-on-the-market-treatment-of-the-piigs-countries-during-the-crisis/.

    Political historian Richard Heffernan writes that Thatcherism became 'the domestic transmission belt for a internationalised [sic] neo-liberalism'. Particularly after 1975, Thatcher's Conservative party 'rema[de] the British political agenda' through 'New Right' policies that included the kind of political restructuring that moved Labour to the right, hence the birth of Blair's New Labour. Heffernan, 2000, *New Labour and Thatcherism: Political Change in Britain*, Palgrave Macmillan, pp. ix–x.

    It is also worth noting that 1975 was the year in which the business group, the Trilateral Commission, published a report on what they called the 'crisis of democracy' affecting North America, Japan, and Western Europe. Their solution to the problem of excessive public engagement in political and economic affairs was to restructure the economies of those societies in order to crush welfare, solidarity and thus social cohesion. (Michel J. Crozier, Samuel P. Huntington and Joji Watanuki, 1975, *The Crisis of Democracy: Report on the Governability of Democracies to the Trilateral Commission*, New York University Press.)

2. In 2016, 1,400 corporate CEOs were surveyed by Pricewaterhouse-Coopers on their major concerns. 79% of CEOs said that 'over-regulation' was their biggest concern. (Tom Levitt, 'Climate change fails to top list of threats for business leaders at Davos', *Guardian*, 20 January 2016, https://www.theguardian.com/sustainable-business/2016/jan/20/climate-change-threats-business-leaders-davos-survey.)

The British public has been consistently opposed to the kind of privatization that defines the neoliberal project. A YouGov poll from 2013, for instance, suggests that 68% of the public, including a majority of those who vote Tory and UKIP, want energy run in the public sector. 66% want the railway services nationalized as do 67% with regards to the postal service. On the issue of public ownership, UKIP voters are mostly left-wing: 78% of UKIP voters want the energy companies nationalized, as do 73% in regards to the railways. This is an even higher percentage than Liberal Democrat voters. (Will Dahlgreen, 'Nationalise energy and rail companies, say public', YouGov, 4 November, 2013, https://yougov.co.uk/news/2013/11/04/nationalise-energy-and-rail-companies-say-public/.)

Furthermore, the record is consistent. In the 2003/4 edition of *British Social Attitudes*, the analysts, having studied 20 years of British social attitudes, conclude that '[s]upport for better public services such as health and education is as high now as it has ever been. The public continues to believe that access to publicly funded health care should be based on need rather than income. It continues to believe as well that financial support for university students should be in the form of grants rather than loans', except where students can afford fees. (Alison Park, John Curtice, Katarina Thomson, Lindsey Jarvis, and Catherine Bromley (eds.), 2003, *British Social Attitudes: Continuity and change over two decades: The 20th report*, SAGE and National Centre for Social Research, p. 256.)

3. On labour rights, two economists at the London School of Economics survey the correlation between neoliberal policies and workers' rights. They find 'a negative relationship between such openness and worker rights. Most directly this implies that efforts to increase participation in the global economy are accompanied by reduced protection for workers. These results provide some support for the oft-raised "race to the bottom" dynamic regarding global capital and labour rights'. (Robert Blanton and Dursun Peksen, 'The dark side of economic freedom: Neoliberalism has deleterious effects on labour rights', LSE, 19 August 2016, http://blogs.lse.ac.uk/politicsandpolicy/the-dark-side-of-economic-freedom/.)

On the future of the neoliberal project: Britain's former Business Secretary, Vince Cable, a former economist at Shell, wrote a paper in 1996 defining the 'new agenda for free trade' across the world, which happens to mirror the old 19th century agenda. (See my *Britain's Secret Wars*, 2016, Clairview Books, pp. 3–4.)

Twenty years on, Springer et al. write that 'neoliberalism has grown exponentially over the past two decades, coinciding with the meteoric rise of this phenomenon as a hegemonic ideology, a state form, a policy and programme'. (Simon Springer, Kean Birch and Julie MacLeavy (eds.), 2016, *The Handbook of Neoliberalism*, Routledge, p. 1.)

4. The Conservative Party Manifesto 2015, p. 30, https://s3-eu-west-1.amazonaws.com/manifesto2015/ConservativeManifesto2015.pdf.

In his autobiography, former Tory PM Ted Heath writes about the necessity of joining the EU's forerunner, the European Economic Community, to promote Britain's global 'capitalist' aspirations: 'More and more politicians ... came to view that Britain's future, like so much of its history, lay in Europe – and that we needed to become part of the European Community, or risk becoming marginal in the development of world economic, monetary and trade relations'. Heath writes that after WWII, 'the Labour government was expending its energies in its programmes of nationalisation ... Ministers thought that [the European Coal and Steel Community, a forerunner to the EEC] would be based on a coalition of non-socialist parties in a capitalist Europe. They were also reluctant to cede control over industries they had only just nationalised'. Attlee's Labour government decided not to join the ECSC. This was 'immensely damaging', Heath opines, hence the Tory government's decision to force Britain into the EEC (which came after the ECSC) without a referendum. (Edward Heath, 2011, *The Course of My Life: My Autobiography*, A&C Black, especially Chapters 8 and 13.)

On Euroscepticism, a pre-Brexit poll by YouGov found that the UK Independence Party 'look[ed] likely to take the largest share of the vote' in the European Parliament. The poll shows an 'increase in support since 2009 for the largest Eurosceptic party in Sweden (Sweden Democrats), Germany (Alternative for Deutschland), Britain (UKIP), Denmark (Danish People's Party), Finland (Finns Party) and France (the Front National)'. The poll goes on to note that 'Britain stands out as the only country where less than a fifth of people rate themselves as very strongly European'. (William Jordan, 'EuroTrack: The swing to the Eurosceptic Right', YouGov, 12 May, 2014, https://yougov.co.uk/news/2014/05/12/swing-eurosceptic-right/.)

5. Ted Bromund and Nile Gardiner, 'Freedom from the EU: Why Britain and U.S. Should Pursue a U.S.–U.K. Free Trade Area', Heritage Foundation, 26 September 2014, http://www.heritage.org/research/reports/2014/09/freedom-from-the-eu-why-britain-and-the-us-should-pursue-a-usuk-free-trade-area.

On US post-war efforts to build a United Europe, see Richard J. Aldrich, 'OSS, CIA and European unity: The American committee on United Europe, 1948–60', *Diplomacy and Statecraft*, 8:1, 1997, pp. 184–227. Aldrich writes that the forerunner to the US Central Intelligence Agency, the Office of Strategic Services, worked hard in Europe, particularly in Britain, to persuade various politicians to favour unification. This went as far as establishing the Committee for a United Europe (ACUE), which was critical of the Labour party and its recalcitrance. Aldrich writes, for example: 'The assumption which underpinned much ACUE thinking was that unification would resolve the old problems of European nationalism', meaning independence from Anglo-American interests, 'reconciling the French and others to the harnessing of German military power. Donovan', the head of the CIA's forerunner, 'favoured the Schuman Plan', for a Franco-German industrial pact,' for these reasons' (p. 192).

6. On the deregulation of the City of London in the 1980s, the so-called Big Bang, former Tory Chancellor, Nigel Lawson, writes: 'Without the reform, it is doubtful if London would have retained its place as Europe's pre-eminent financial centre, and certain that it would not have become the foremost truly international financial centre of the modern, globalised economy that it is today'. On the financialization, which has so harmed the real economy, Lawson writes: 'in the securities market [Britain] was in danger of becoming a backwater. And there was no way in which London could remain a world-class financial centre without a world-class securities business'. Lawson laments the 'predictable outrage from the Labour Party', which then still represented irrelevant interests, namely the general public: a problem overcome with the rise of New Labour. Lawson concludes that US regulation, which affects the London Stock Exchange on account of a large amount of US ownership in London, and the EU's increasing, pre-Crisis regulation, 'need resolutely to be resisted'. See Lawson et al. (eds.), *The Big Bang 20 years on: New challenges facing the financial services sector: Collected Essays*, 2006, Centre for Policy Studies, pp. i–iii, https://www.cps.org.uk/files/reports/original/111028101637-20061019EconomyBigBang20YearsOn.pdf.

On hedge funds specifically, 'Since the late 1990s there has been a marked increase in the allocation of funds by institutional investors, their global holdings rising from 25% in 1997 to 37% in 2006. In the United States, the source of 65% of hedge fund assets in 2006, institutional investors now generate 40% of hedge fund investment. Europe is the source of 24% of hedge fund assets and Asia 8%'. (Richard Roberts, 2008 (2nd), *The City: A Guide to London's Global Financial Centre*, Profile Books and The Economist, p. 156.)

Asia's low hedge fund concentration will likely reverse after Brexit as Britain will seek to capture the markets of China, India and South Korea, mainly with US capital which uses the City of London as a safe offshore haven to effectively launder its money and immunize US investors from crashes. For the Citigroup report, see Citigroup, 'Opportunities and Challenges for Hedge Funds in the Coming Era of Optimization: Part 1: Changes Driven by the Investor Audience', Citi Investor Services, no date, http://www.citibank.com/icg/global_markets/prime_finance/docs/Opportunities_and_Challenges_for_Hedge_Funds_in_the_Coming_Era_of_Optimization.pdf.

7. Sources and details are provided throughout this book.

8. On protectionism in post-Crisis Europe, Pieter Cleppe of the right-wing Open Europe think-tank laments 'the forces of protectionism gaining ground both at national and EU level', including stalling on trade deals with the USA and raising tariffs on aluminium to reach environmental targets. (Cleppe, 'Regulation, then protectionism: Is Europe going the way of its aluminium sector?', EurActiv.com, 17 June 2016, https://www.euractiv.com/section/trade-society/opinion/regulation-then-protectionism-is-europe-going-the-way-of-its-aluminium-sector/.)

The European Commission's 2014 report on trade restrictions concluded that 850 protectionist measures were raised since the financial crisis, mainly in China, India, Indonesia and Russia, but also in the EU itself. (Benjamin Fox, 'Trade protectionism still on the rise, EU research finds', EU Observer, 18 November 2014, https://euobserver.com/news/126559.)

In 2012, the UK think-tank, Overseas Development Institute (ODI), found that '[t]he trade reforms that the EU is pushing through currently are ones that increase rather than reduce trade barriers'. The EU is also 'complaining of the protectionist stances of other G20 countries'. It is worth noting that ODI says that Europe's approach to investing in and trading with the 'developing world' 'lacks vision'. (ODI, 'Creeping protectionism in EU trade policy', 26 July 2012, https://www.odi.org/news/604-eu-trade-policy-international-development-global-challenges.)

It is also worth noting who funds the ODI: funders include the right-wing, pro-neoliberal Adam Smith International, the Asia Development Bank, the Bill and Melinda Gates Foundation, the European Union, Mastercard Foundation, the Rockefeller Foundation and the World

Bank (https://www.odi.org/sites/odi.org.uk/files/downloads/1_odi_funders.pdf).

On the roots of neoliberalism, see Arthur John Taylor, 1972, *Laissez-faire and state intervention in nineteenth-century Britain*, Macmillan. Ivan Berend, 2013, *An Economic History of Nineteenth-Century Europe: Diversity and Industrialization*, Cambridge University Press. David Harvey, 2007, *A Brief History of Neoliberalism*, Oxford University Press.

9. On government insurance policies before and after the Crisis, see Gary H. Stern and Ron J. Feldman, 2004, *Too Big to Fail: The Hazards of Bank Bailouts*, Brookings Institution. Josh Bivens, 2011, *Failure by Design: The Story behind America's Broken Economy*, Economic Policy Institute. Neil Barofsky, 2012, *Bailout: An Inside Account of How Washington Abandoned Main Street While Rescuing Wall Street*, Simon and Schuster.

10. Lynsey Barber, 'Sunday Times Rich List 2016: The number of billionaires in London has fallen, but it's still the super-rich capital of the world', City A.M., 24 April 2016, http://www.cityam.com/239517/sunday-times-rich-list-2016-the-number-of-billionaires-in-london-has-fallen-but-its-still-the-super-rich-capital-of-the-world. Richard Keen and Ross Turner, 'Statistics on migrants and benefits', House of Commons Library, Briefing Paper Number CBP 7445, 8 February 2016, www.parliament.uk/briefing-papers/SN06955.pdf. James Denman and Paul McDonald, 'Unemployment statistics from 1881 to the present day', *Labour Market Trends*, Government Statistical Service (Office of National Statistics), January, 1996, pp. 8–18, www.ons.gov.uk/ons/rel/lms/labour-market.../unemployment-since-1881.pdf.

11. Bojan Bugaric, 'Europe Against the Left? On Legal Limits to Progressive Politics', London School of Economics, LSE, Europe in Question Discussion Paper Series, LEQS Paper No. 61/2013, May 2013, http://www.lse.ac.uk/europeanInstitute/LEQS%20Discussion%20Paper%20Series/LEQSPaper61.pdf.

12. Mark A. Pollack, 'A Blairite Treaty: Neo-Liberalism and Regulated Capitalism in the Treaty of Amsterdam' in Karlheinz Neunreither and Antje Wiener (eds.), 2000, *European Integration After Amsterdam*, Oxford University Press, pp. 273–74.

13. Robert E. Bohrer and Alexander C. Tan, 'Left Turn in Europe? Reactions to Austerity and the EMU', *Political Research Quarterly*, September, 2000, 53:3, pp. 575–595.

14. The masses of data and analysis on propaganda rarely yield results on whether or not it is successful. In a rare study, Reeves et al. summarize that one of Britain's leading tabloids, *The Sun* (owned by Rupert Murdoch), made political 'endorsements [which] were associated with a significant increase in readers' support for [Tony Blair's New] Labour in 1997, approximately 525,000 votes, and its switch back was associated with about 550,000 extra votes for the Conservatives in 2010'. The confusion among voting readers of *The Sun* correlates with other polling analyses which suggest that a significant percentage of voters are undecided until relatively late in a given election or referendum (Brexit included) and that even among Conservative voters there is a high percentage who, like their left-wing counterparts, endorse socialist principles, including nationalization. See Aaron Reeves, Martin McKee and David Stuckler, ' "It's *The Sun* Wot Won It": Evidence of media influence on political attitudes and voting from a UK quasi-natural experiment', *Social Science Research*, 56, 2016, pp. 44–57.

It is also worth noting that hedge funds, many of which supported Brexit, invest in Rupert Murdoch's media, *The Sun* being one of the only pro-Brexit papers in the UK. For example: Lynsey Barber, '21st Century Fox: ValueAct Capital takes $1bn stake in Murdoch's entertainment company', City A.M., 12 August 2014, http://www.cityam.com/1407834712/21st-century-fox-valueact-capital-takes-1bn-stake-murdoch-s-entertainment-company.

15. On the vagueness of 'globalization', consider a post-Crisis Eurobarometer poll. 55% of Britons thought that 'globalization' (not clearly defined in the poll) can bring economic growth, compared with 16% who didn't. The relatively high support for 'globalization', which declined in light of the crash of 2007 and Euro-wide austerity of post-2009, indicates that people enjoy trading with foreign neighbours and are internationalists by nature. (European Commission, 'Public Opinion in the European Union', Standard Eurobarometer 79, Spring

2013, p. 82, http://ec.europa.eu/public_opinion/archives/eb/eb79/eb79_publ_en.pdf.)

Consider also a Pew poll, which finds that 81% of global respondents think that '[t]rade is good', 74% who feel that '[f]oreign companies building in our country is good', and that '[t]rade creates jobs'. However, when the public learns the details of what this form of 'globalization' involves, support declines. 45% think that '[t]rade raises wages' and 26% think that '[t]rade decreases prices'. (Pew Research Center, 'Faith and Skepticism about Trade, Foreign Investment', 16 September 2014, http://www.pewglobal.org/2014/09/16/faith-and-skepticism-about-trade-foreign-investment/.)

The same polling agency finds broad support for a Free Trade Agreement between Europe and the USA: 74% in the Netherlands, 71% in Ireland and Denmark, 65% in the UK, 63% in Spain, and even higher percentages in many Eastern European countries. (Bruce Stokes, 'Is Europe on board for a new trade deal with the U.S.?', Pew Research Center, 29 January 2015, http://www.pewresearch.org/fact-tank/2015/01/29/is-europe-on-board-for-a-new-trade-deal-with-the-u-s/.)

However, again, when people learn what exactly 'free trade' and this particular form of globalization involves, enthusiasm tends to wane, with 97% of 150,000 European respondents opposing the new EU-US 'free trade' deal, the Transatlantic Trade and Investment Partnership, particularly its inclusion of legal provisions that will allow governments to be sued by corporations and wealthy individuals for impeding their profits by, for instance, raising working standards, blocking privatization, or protecting the environment. (Chatham House, 'TTIP: Shaping the Future of Investor-State Dispute Settlement?', 4 March 2015, https://www.chathamhouse.org/event/ttip-shaping-future-investor-state-dispute-settlement.)

16. Lord Ashcroft polls, 'How the United Kingdom voted on Thursday … and why', 24 June 2016, http://lordashcroftpolls.com/2016/06/how-the-united-kingdom-voted-and-why/.

17. Ibid.

18. Ibid.

19. Ibid.

20. Ibid.

21. The British Chamber of Commerce stated prior to the referendum that 54% of its 2,200 members were backing Remain: a downward trend of six percentage points from the preceding month. This was partly due to the propaganda of Leave and also the sense of which way the wind was blowing among the richest businesses. 10% of business leaders said they were undecided/could be swayed. (BBC News Online, 'EU referendum: BCC says businesses back Remain but gap narrows', 10 May 2016, http://www.bbc.co.uk/news/uk-politics-eu-referendum-36252315.)

On bank–hedge fund rivalry, the *Financial Times* reported prior to the Financial Crisis that '[b]ig hedge funds have recently grabbed such a large share of trading in US Treasury bonds that their activity is eclipsing many of the investment banks that have traditionally dominated the market'. The use of algorithms by hedge funds to detect price fluctuations and beat human resource traders 'has fuelled unease among banks about requests the hedge funds are making to become direct participants in the eurozone government bond market'. (Richard Beales and Gillian Tett, 'Hedge funds rival banks for share of US Treasury market', *FT*, 9 March 2007.)

22. The more the pound weakens, the more it strengthens investors in other currencies: 'Corporations often talk about how foreign exchange impacts them. Apple, for example, said in January that overseas revenue worth $100 in the last quarter of 2014 was worth just $85 in the first quarter of 2016, after it was translated back to a dollar. The reason? A stronger dollar'. This is the opinion of two analysts writing for the *Wall Street Journal*. They conclude: 'A weakening pound will have the opposite impact on U.K. multinationals. Most of their sales come from abroad but are reported in sterling. In the case of companies in the FTSE 100 stock index, three quarters of their revenues are international and will suddenly look much beefier in the eyes of investors when they are converted into pounds. This is one of the reasons the FTSE 100 has held its ground after Brexit'. (Jon Sindreu and Ben Eisen, 'Why does a weak pound matter to the world?', *WSJ*, 28

June 2016, http://blogs.wsj.com/moneybeat/2016/06/28/why-does-a-weak-pound-matter-to-the-world/).

23. See Chapters 2, 3, and 4.

Introduction

1. Ted Bromund and Nile Gardiner, 'Freedom from the EU: Why Britain and U.S. Should Pursue a U.S.-U.K. Free Trade Area', Heritage Foundation, 26 September 2014, http://www.heritage.org/research/reports/2014/09/freedom-from-the-eu-why-britain-and-the-us-should-pursue-a-usuk-free-trade-area.

2. Rosie Goldsmith, 'Profile: Nigel Farage, UKIP leader', BBC Radio 4, 4 December 2012, BBC News Online, http://www.bbc.co.uk/news/uk-politics-20543513. Farage's father and brother were City brokers. Farage himself worked for RJ Rouse & Co., before setting up Farage Futures. He then founded commodities brokerage, Farage Limited. (Henry Sanderson, 'Nigel Farage's pinstriped image belies modest City career', *Financial Times*, 6 February 2015.)

On HIV-AIDS, Farage said back in 2014 that the kind of immigrants he would allow into the country would be '[p]eople who do not have HIV, to be frank. That's a good start. And people with a skill'. (Nicholas Watt, 'Keep HIV-positive migrants out of Britain, says UKIP's Nigel Farage', *Guardian*, 10 October 2014, http://www.theguardian.com/politics/2014/oct/10/nigel-farage-keep-hiv-positive-migrants-out-britain.) During the election campaign 2015, Farage said: 'There are seven thousand diagnoses in this country every year for people who are HIV-positive, which is not a good place for any of them to be, I know. But sixty percent of them are not British nationals. You can come into Britain from anywhere in the world and get diagnosed with HIV and get the retroviral drugs that cost up to £25,000 per year, per patient. I know there are some horrible things happening in many parts of the world, but what we need to do is to put the National Health Service there for British people and families, who, in many cases, have paid into this system for decades'. (Sky News, 'Leaders' Debate – Nigel Farage On HIV and the NHS', YouTube, 2 April 2015, https://www.youtube.com/watch?v=2m9S1PCiuEs.) As late as June

2016, Farage was holding fast to his AIDS policy, telling the BBC that people with HIV-AIDS 'would be a huge burden on the [National] Health Service ... It's a national health service. It's not an international health service'. See BBC News, 'Nigel Farage: Voters 'beginning to put two fingers up' to PM', YouTube, 12 June 2016, https://www.youtube.com/watch?v=rk73t-OBEpc.

Tariq Ali '[said] that the majority of British voters gave the EU "a big kick in its backside," explaining that the majority of working class "leave" voters felt that overall the EU did not benefit them, was undemocratic and an organization for the rich and the banks'. (tele-SUR, 'Tariq Ali "Pleased" Brexit Has Given EU "Big Kick" up "Back-side"', 24 June 2016, http://www.telesurtv.net/english/news/Tariq-Ali-Pleased-Brexit-Has-Given-EU-Big-Kick-up-Backside-20160624-0033.html.)

3. Owen Jones, 'Grieve now if you must – but prepare for the great challenges ahead...', *Guardian*, 24 June 2016. On the questions over Jones's socialism, consider his remarks on restructuring society and business: 'power needs to be devolved away from Westminster to local councils, including in areas such as housing, education and health'. Banks love these words because devolution opens the door to privatization, as Jones appears to acknowledge: 'Rather than [selling] the banks that were bailed out by the taxpayer, government could turn these institutions into publicly owned regional investment banks, helping to rebuild local economies across Britain'. This is not socialism, Jones assures us, as it 'does not mean entirely replicating a top-down statist model'. Jones is not concerned with genuine worker ownership, but with the illusion of ownership and participation: 'Allowing service users to feel that these services are *theirs*, democratically owned by *them*, would do exactly that' (emphases in original). Notice that Jones doesn't say the services would be theirs, but that workers would 'feel' they were. (Owen Jones, 2014, *The Establishment and How They Get Away with It*, Allen Lane, pp. 306–7, 312.)

On Cameron's state-crimes against social security recipients, Department for Work and Pensions figures released under the Freedom of Information Act reveal that at least 2,380 individuals died after their entitlements were stopped in the government's budget cuts. Initially, the Department refused to release the figures, but were compelled to after intervention by the Information Commissioner. The figures include the period December 2011 to February 2014 and equate to approximately 90 deaths per month. (BBC News Online, 'More than 2,300 died after fit for work assessment – DWP figures', 27 August 2015, http://www.bbc.co.uk/news/uk-34074557.) Victims include persons driven to suicide, including 30-year-old Leanne Chambers, and army veterans, including David Clapson, who died after his insulin could not be refrigerated because benefit cuts prevented him from paying his electricity bills. (Calum's List, 'Welfare Reform Deaths – Memorial Pages', no date, http://calumslist.org/.)

4. These include the EU's Working Time Directive (2003/88/EC), which 'requires EU countries to guarantee the following rights for all workers: a limit to weekly working hours . . . a minimum daily rest period . . . a rest during working hours . . . a minimum weekly rest . . . paid annual leave . . . extra protection for night work . . . free health assessments [for night workers]'. (European Commission, 'Working Conditions – Working Time Directive', Employment, Social Affairs and Inclusion, http://ec.europa.eu/social/
main.jsp?catId=706&langId=en&intPageId=205.)

On the Treaty of Rome, for instance: 'Although article 222 . . . requires that policies adopted by the European institutions remain neutral with respect to member states' choice of type of ownership (private or public) of their enterprises, in practice few SOEs [state-owned enterprises] are likely to be able to resist the onslaught of competition and the greater efficiency it requires'. (Pierre Guislain, 1997, *The Privatization Challenge: A Strategic, Legal, and Institutional Analysis of International Experience*, World Bank, p. 235.)

The same applies to the Maastricht Treaty. Future Deputy Director General for European Economic Monetary Issues, Dr Camilla Schloenbach, wrote: 'structural deficiencies' in the EEC 'constitute an obstacle to growth. They are to be found in particular in the lack of flexibility in wages and prices and in an excessive government presence in trade and industry. Deregulation and privatization are suitable means of tackling this problem' ('Germany' in Aaron Wild-avsky and Eduardo Zapico-Goñi (eds.), 1993, *National Budgeting for Economic and Monetary Union*, Martinus Nijhoff Publishers, pp. 189–90.)

5. For instance: InfoWars.com, 'Brexit! Britain votes to leave the EU – Globalists defeated!', Sky News, 23 June, 2016, http://www.infowars.com/brexit-britain-votes-to-leave-the-eu-globalists-defeated/.

There is some truth to the 'new world order' objective. When Britain was the global power, it wanted every country and every people to follow its wishes. Even as the Empire declined, the British establishment tried to form a global system of rules that would enable the UK to retain sovereignty while making other nations surrender theirs. This was the League of Nations. (On Britain's intentions, see Carroll Quigley, 1981 [1949], *The Anglo-American Establishment: From Rhodes to Cliveden*, GSG and Associates, pp. 254–55. On the continuation of this policy and its migration to US imperial interests, see Sir Laurence Martin, 'Chatham House at 75: The Past, Present and Future', *International Affairs*, 74:1, October 1995, pp. 697–703.)

On austerity, three IMF economists, for instance, write: 'removing restrictions on the movement of capital across a country's borders (so-called capital account liberalization); and fiscal consolidation, sometimes called "austerity," which is shorthand for policies to reduce fiscal deficits and debt levels' have resulting in: '[t]he benefits in terms of increased growth seem[ing] fairly difficult to establish when looking at a broad group of countries. – The costs in terms of increased inequality are prominent. Such costs epitomize the trade-off between the growth and equity effects of some aspects of the neoliberal agenda ... Increased inequality in turn hurts the level and sustainability of growth'. (Jonathan D. Ostry, Prakash Loungani and Davide Furceri, 'Neoliberalism: Oversold?', *Finance and Development*, 53:2, June 2016, http://www.imf.org/external/pubs/ft/fandd/2016/06/ostry.htm.)

Despite these and much earlier warnings against austerity, the so-called Troika (IMF, ECB and EC) continued its policies, as did the British government separately from Brussels.

6. For example, in the mainstream, Philip Johnston, 'Do you want sovereignty back? Then vote to leave the EU', *Telegraph*, 8 February 2016, http://www.telegraph.co.uk/news/newstopics/eureferendum/12146990/Do-you-want-sovereignty-back-Then-vote-to-leave-the-EU.html and, in the alternative media, David Icke, 'The Brexit Vote. What Does it Mean? Hopefully, a Breakup of the EU and NATO, the Avoidance of World War III', 25 June 2016, https://www.davidicke.com/article/376170/brexit-vote-mean-hopefully-breakup-eu-nato-avoidance-world-war-iii.

7. 'Awkward partner' was a phrase popularized in academia by Stephen George, who writes: 'British government attitudes have been influenced at least as much by a commitment on the part of the political and administrative elites to a wider, global internationalism as they have by considerations of nationalism, and that any appearance of following the line of the United States is simply due to the general commitment of governments in both countries to this global outlook'. This finds commonality with the sentiments expressed in endnote 5 on the 'new world order'. George continues: 'British governments ... have been concerned to avoid the emergence of an inward-looking EC that would form a regional bloc relatively isolated from the rest of the capitalist world system'. This chimes with Bromund and Gardiner (endnote 1, above), who call Britain, America's 'Trojan Horse' in Europe. It is also reflected in post-Brexit policy, as Chapters 2, 3 and 4 demonstrate. (Stephen George, 'British policy in the European Community: The Commitment to Globalism', University of Sheffield, 1991, http://aei.pitt.edu/7230/1/002478_1.pdf.)

   For details of the Factortame case, see Books LLC, 2010, *European Union Legal Cases: Factortame Litigation, Webster Ruling, European Union Microsoft Competition Case, Apostolides V Orams*, Books LLC.

8. On New Labour's dismantling of workers' rights, Cambridge economist William Brown concludes: 'The Labour Party had long been heavily dependent on the trade unions financially – 75 per cent of its funds came from them in 1985 – and knew that it could not look business-friendly and independent unless it broke that link. By 2002, New Labour had found alternative sources of finance and only 30 per

cent of its funds came from the unions'. Williams thinks that unions reconciled with New Labour after 2005, which is a dubious assertion. See William Brown, 'Industrial Relations in Britain under New Labour, 1997–2010: A post mortem', January 2011, CWPE 1121, p. 9, http://www.econ.cam.ac.uk/dae/repec/cam/pdf/cwpe1121.pdf. On austerity as choice, see William Keegan, 2014, *Mr. Osborne's Economic Experiment: Austerity 1945–57 and 2010–*, Searching Finance Limited. Craig Berry, 2016, *Austerity Politics and UK Economic Policy*, Springer. Janan Ganesh, 2014, *George Osborne: The Austerity Chancellor*, Biteback Publishing.

On Greece, see Georgios Karyotis and Roman Gerodimos, 2015, *The Politics of Extreme Austerity: Greece in the Eurozone Crisis*, Springer.

9. European Union Committee, 'Chapter 3: Fiscal Discipline', *The future of economic governance in the EU: Twelfth Report, House of Lords*, 22 March 2011, http://www.publications.parliament.uk/pa/ld201011/ldselect/ldeucom/124/12406.htm.

10. Council of the European Union, 'UK's block opt-out and partial re-opt-in to the ex-third pillar acquis', Press Release, 1 December 2014, http://www.consilium.europa.eu/uedocs/cms_data/docs/pressdata/en/jha/145981.pdf and Lords Select Committee, 'Lords question Home Secretary and Justice Secretary on UK opt-in', 14 January 2015, http://www.parliament.uk/business/committees/committees-a-z/lords-select/eu-law-and-institutions-sub-committee-e/news/jha-opt-in-hsec-jsec-eveupdate/.

11. Robin Niblett, 'Britain, the EU and the Sovereignty Myth', Chatham House, May 2016, https://www.chathamhouse.org/sites/files/chathamhouse/publications/research/2016-05-09-britain-eu-sovereignty-myth-niblett-final.pdf.

12. Ibid.

13. Markus W. Gehring, 'Brexit and EU-UK trade relations with third states', EU Law Analysis, 6 March 2016, http://eulawanalysis.blogspot.co.uk/2016/03/brexit-and-eu-uk-trade-relations-with.html and Ruth Lea, 'After Brexit, access to EFTA's suite of trade agreements would be an economic boost', London School of

Economics and Political Science, 22 June 2016, http://blogs.lse.ac.uk/brexit/2016/06/22/in-case-of-a-brexit-access-to-eftas-suite-of-trade-agreements-would-be-an-economic-boost/.

14. Michel Boutillier and Jean Cordier, for instance, find that France deregulated a decade later than the UK (2003, *Economic Modelling at the Banque de France: Financial Deregulation and Economic Development in France*, Routledge).

   On Brazil, Russia, India and China, see Vai Io Lo and Mary Hiscock (eds.), 2014, *The Rise of the BRICS in the Global Political Economy: Changing Paradigms?*, Edward Elgar Publishing.

   Long before the 2008 Crisis, austerity and growing protectionism, many economists were lamenting Europe's sluggish growth, seemingly unaware that the very neoliberal programmes they preach were the underlying cause. See, for instance, Vice Chairman of Goldman Sachs Europe, Guillermo de la Dehesa, 2006, *Europe at the Crossroads: Will the EU be Able to Compete with the United States as an Economic Power?*, McGraw-Hill. Dehesa's conclusion, that Europe needs to be more like the US and Britain, i.e., surrender its markets to neoliberal internationalism, has a great deal of implication for the rest of the world, namely that the US seeks to expand its ideological and economic power over Europe in order to act as a Leviathan forcing Asia and Africa to conform to its favoured model in order to compete.

15. Gehring, op. cit.

16. Ibid.

17. Lea, op. cit.

18. Peter Lilley, 'The truth about Britain's trade outside the European Union', *Telegraph*, 26 May 2016, http://www.telegraph.co.uk/news/2016/05/26/the-truth-about-britains-trade-outside-the-european-union/.

   On Lilley's 'Mikado' speech and verbal attacks on 'young ladies who get pregnant, just to jump the housing queue', 'new-age travellers' and 'bogus asylum seekers', see jascow0, 'Peter Lilley speech to Tory conference 1992 – "I have a little list"', 18 October 2012, https://www.youtube.com/watch?v=FOx8q3eGq3g. Mark Lawson, 'The making of our blue Peter', *Independent*, 2 April 1994,

http://www.independent.co.uk/arts-entertainment/the-making-of-
blue-peter-in-the-last-two-years-peter-lilley-has-shot-from-obscurity-to-
euro-baiting-1367591.html.

19. Lilley, op. cit.
20. Niblett, op. cit.
21. EFTA, 'Persons', no date,
    http://www.efta.int/eea/policy-areas/persons/persons. The website
    states that the Agreement includes the EU: 'Free movement of persons
    is one of the core freedoms of the European Internal Market. This area
    is covered by Article 28 of the [European Economic Area] Agreement,
    Annex V on the Free Movement of Workers and Annex VIII on the
    Right of Establishment. Accordingly, nationals of the EEA EFTA States
    (Iceland, Norway and Liechtenstein) have the same right as EU citizens
    to take up an economic activity anywhere in the EU/EEA without being
    discriminated against on the grounds of their nationality. Equally, EU
    citizens have the right to work and reside in the EEA EFTA States. Non-
    economically active persons such as pensioners, students and family
    members of EEA nationals are also entitled to move and reside any-
    where in the EU/EEA subject to certain conditions as set out in the
    relevant EU legislation'.
22. Raoul Ruparel, Stephen Booth and Vincenzo Scarpetta, 'Brexit guide:
    What next?', Open Europe, 2016, http://openeurope.org.uk/
    intelligence/britain-and-the-eu/guide-to-brexit/.
23. Ibid. My examples.
24. Ibid.

Chapter 1

1. Economics professor Moritz Schularick notes that this generalizes
   across Europe: 'In the three decades after WW2, between 1945 and
   1974, not a single systemic banking crisis occurred. After this long,
   crisis-free interlude, the crisis frequency increased again in recent
   decades. The high incidence of banking crisis in the late 19th and early
   20th century might partly be explained by insufficient liquidity provision and the absence of Lender of Last Resort actions by the central
   banks. But this does not help to explain the high incidence of banking

crises in the past 30 years. Other factors – financial deregulation and international capital market integration come to mind – must have also played a role'. (Schularick, '140 years of financial crises: Old dog, new tricks', August 2010, http://www.jfki.fu-berlin.de/faculty/economics/team/Ehemalige_Mitarbeiter_innen/schularick/Old_Dog_New_Tricks_Schularick.pdf.)

On the latter (integration), consider how the markets were integrated to such an extent that the US housing bubble nearly brought down the euro.

On wages, see Bill Osgerby, ' "Seized by Change, Liberated by Affluence": Youth, Consumption and Cultural Change in Post-war Britain' in Bob Moore and Hank van Nierop (eds.), *Twentieth-century Mass Society in Britain and the Netherlands*, Berg. Providing no counter-evidence, Osgerby writes that Mark Abrams popularized the idea of post-war prosperity among the young, writing that the figures were 'probably exaggerated ... but notions of "affluent youth" had a degree of foundation' (p. 178).

On income inequality, the 'UK had falling inequality from 1945 to late 1970s ... In the UK, overall inequality levelled off since 1990', largely due to massive inequality in the 1980s which remained into the 1990s, 'but top shares continued to rise [among the 1% and particularly the 0.05%]'. See A.B. Atkinson, 'Income inequality in historical and comparative perspective', GINI Project, March 2010, http://www.gini-research.org/system/uploads/19/original/Atkinson_GINI_Mar2010_.pdf?1269619027.

2. Quotes and background in Robin Ramsay, 'Well, how did we get here?', *Lobster Magazine*, 60, Winter 2010, http://www.lobster-magazine.co.uk/free/lobster60/lob60-062.pdf.

3. Preqin, 'Four-Fifths of Europe-Based Hedge Fund Managers Believe Britain will Remain in the EU', 16 June 2016, https://www.preqin.com/docs/press/Hedge-Funds-Brexit.pdf.

4. Jonathan Cribb, 'Income inequality in the UK', Institute for Fiscal Studies, 2013, http://www.ifs.org.uk/docs/ER_JC_2013.pdf.

5. Ajay Kapur, Niall Macleod and Narendra Singh, 'Plutonomy: Buying Luxury, Explaining Global Imbalances', Equity Strategy, Citigroup, 16

October 2005 and Kapur et al., 'Revisiting Plutonomy: The Rich Getting Richer', Equity Strategy, Citigroup, 5 March 2006.

6. The Financial Crisis Inquiry Commission, 2011, *The Financial Crisis Inquiry Report: Final Report of the National Commission on the Causes of the Financial and Economic Crisis in the United States*, Government Printing Office.

On the recent historical uses of austerity as a forerunner to privatization, Andrew Glyn writes that 1970s' and 80s' America 'saw tight monetary policy and fiscal austerity imposed in the name of defeating inflation ... Privatization, and the deregulation of the industries concerned', primarily the financial sector, 'and the deregulation of labour markets are all aspects of this process'. (Glyn, 2006, *Capitalism Unleashed: Finance, Globalization, and Welfare*, Oxford University Press, pp. 24–25.)

7. For example, Gerard Caprio, 'Financial Regulation After the Crisis: How Did We Get Here, and How Do We Get Out?', London School of Economics Financial Markets Group Special Paper Series, Special Paper 226, November 2013, http://www.lse.ac.uk/fmg/workingPapers/specialPapers/PDF/sp226.pdf.

8. HM Government, 'Review of the Balance of Competences between the United Kingdom and the European Union: The Single Market', July 2013, The Stationery Office, p. 52.

9. Ibid, p. 53.

10. European Commission, 'Updated rules for markets in financial instruments: MiFID 2', Banking and Finance, http://ec.europa.eu/finance/securities/isd/mifid2/index_en.htm.

11. TaylorWessing, 'The Alternative Investment Fund Managers Directive ('AIFIMD')', 2012, https://united-kingdom.taylorwessing.com/fileadmin/files/docs/The-Alternative-Investment-Fund-Managers-Directive.pdf.

12. Michael Bow, 'EU referendum: Hedge fund managers backing "Out" campaign set to make millions from Brexit', *Independent*, 25 October 2015, http://www.independent.co.uk/news/uk/politics/eu-referendum-hedge-fund-managers-backing-out-campaign-set-to-make-millions-from-brexit-a6708496.html. PwC, 'AIFMD: Hedge Fund

managers will face significant changes', no date,
http://www.pwc.co.uk/industries/financial-services/regulation/
aifmd/hedge-fund-managers-must-make-changes-to-comply-with-the-
alternative-investment-fund-managers-directive-aifmd.html.

13. Quoted in Ted Bromund and Nile Gardiner, 'Freedom from the EU:
Why Britain and U.S. Should Pursue a U.S.-U.K. Free Trade Area',
Heritage Foundation, 26 September 2014, http://www.heritage.org/
research/reports/2014/09/freedom-from-the-eu-why-britain-and-the-
us-should-pursue-a-usuk-free-trade-area.

14. HM Government, 'The Coalition: our programme for government',
May 2010, Cabinet Office, pp. 19–20.

15. Parliament, 'United Kingdom Borders (Control and Sovereignty) Bill
2015–16', 2015, http://services.parliament.uk/bills/2015-16/
unitedkingdombordercontrolandsovereignty.html.

16. William Hague, 'Review of the Balance of Competences between the
United Kingdom and the European Union', Cm 8415, July 2012,
https://www.gov.uk/government/uploads/system/uploads/
attachment_data/file/35431/eu-balance-of-competences-review.pdf.

17. The Conservative Party Manifesto 2015, p. 72, https://s3-eu-west-
1.amazonaws.com/manifesto2015/ConservativeManifesto2015.pdf.

18. Paul Marshall, 'Hedge funds seek refuge from unfair European regulations', FT, 28 February 2016.

19. Mads Dagnis Jensen & Holly Snaith, 'When politics prevails: the
political economy of a Brexit', Journal of European Public Policy, 2016,
DOI: 10.1080/13501763.2016.1174531.

20. Bow, op. cit.

21. Jim Pickard and Miles Johnson, 'Hedge fund leader Hintze eyes
"generous" Brexit donation', Financial Times, 1 November 2015.

22. George Soros, 'The Brexit crash will make all of you poorer – be
warned', Guardian, 20 June 2016. Antoine Gara, 'How billionaire
George Soros profited from Brexit's "Black Friday"', Forbes, 28 June
2016, http://www.forbes.com/sites/antoinegara/2016/06/28/
how-billionaire-george-soros-profited-from-brexits-black-friday/
#4a8478301e2a.

23. Laurence Fletcher, 'U.K. Hedge Funds Are Loudly Divided on

"Brexit"', *Wall Street Journal*, 19 June 2016, http://www.wsj.com/articles/u-k-hedge-funds-are-loudly-divided-on-brexit-1466368876.

24. Electoral Commission, 'Donations and loans received by campaigners in the European Union Referendum: First pre-poll report: 1 February 2016 to 21 April 2016', http://www.electoralcommission.org.uk/__data/assets/pdf_file/0015/204081/Pre-poll-1-Summary-Document.pdf.

25. David Hellier, 'Why are hedge funds supporting Brexit?', *Guardian*, 6 November 2015.

26. Ibid.

27. Keith Gladdis, Arthur Martin and Richard Pendlebury, 'Hedge fund baron Hintze – sugar daddy to Cameron and Co.', *Daily Mail*, 18 October 2011.

28. Pickard and Johnson, op. cit.

29. Electoral Commission, op. cit.

30. *Financial Times*, 'Toscafund: UK would be "better" for leaving EU', 15 February 2016, www.ft.com/fastft/2016/02/15/toscafund-uk-would-be-better-place-for-leaving-eu/.

31. Fletcher, op. cit.

32. Electoral Commission, op. cit.

33. BBC News Online, 'EU referendum: More than 1,280 business leaders sign letter', 22 June 2016, www.bbc.co.uk/news/business-36592782.

34. Letters, 'Britain's competitiveness is undermined by a failing EU', *Telegraph*, 15 May 2016, http://www.telegraph.co.uk/opinion/2016/05/15/letters-britains-competitiveness-is-undermined-by-a-failing-eu/.

35. Edmond de Rothschild, 'Brexit is a game changer for hedge funds', 19 July 2016, http://www.edmond-de-rothschild.com/site/bahamas/en/news/private-banking/7099-brexit-is-a-game-changer-for-hedge-funds.

36. Electoral Commission, op. cit.

37. Ibid.

38. Ibid.

39. Julia Finch, 'Caudwell sells up and sails away with £1.24bn', *Guardian*, 7 August 2006 and Letters, op. cit.

40. Leave.eu, website.

41. Bruges Group, http://www.brugesgroup.com/.

42. Lobbywatch.org, 'Profiles: Martin Durkin', no date, http://www.lobbywatch.org/profile1.asp?PrId=39.

43. Preqin, op. cit.

44. Will Wainewright, Nishant Kumar and Saijel Kishan, 'Brexit winners emerge in hedge-fund community amid market chaos', *Bloomberg*, 24 June 2016, http://www.bloomberg.com/news/articles/2016-06-24/ brexit-winners-emerge-in-hedge-fund-community-amid-market-chaos. Jemima Kelly and Maiya Keidan, 'Man versus machine: computer-driven hedge funds win on Brexit night', Reuters, 15 July 2016, http://www.reuters.com/article/us-britain-eu-hedgefunds-idUSKCN0ZV27V. Rob Copeland, Gregory Zuckerman and Laurence Fletcher, 'Some hedge funds clean up after Brexit', 25 June 2016, http://www.wsj.com/articles/the-giant-hedge-fund-that-got-brexit-right-1466785809.

45. Odey quoted in ibid. Reuters, 'Computer-driven hedge funds beat human managers on Brexit night', 18 July 2016. Antoine Gara, 'How billionaire George Soros profited from Brexit's "Black Friday"', op. cit. Nishant Kumar, 'Cohen's Point72 says London expansion on track despite Brexit', *Bloomberg*, 26 June 2016, http://www.bloomberg.com/ news/articles/2016-06-26/cohen-s-point72-says-london-expansion-on-track-despite-brexit.

46. Rachael Levy, 'A select group of hedge funds made some serious money on Brexit', *Business Insider*, 25 June 2016, http://uk.businessinsider.com/hedge-funds-trading-on-brexit-2016-6 and Copeland et al., op. cit.

47. *Compass*, 'Tune out the noise', Q1, 2016, Barclays, https://wealth.barclays.com/en_gb/home/research/research-centre/ compass/compass-q1-16/tune-out-the-noise.html.

48. JPMorgan, 'Brexit: Fund Manager Insights', 24 June 2016, https://am.jpmorgan.com/blob-gim/1383351379445/83456/ Brexit%20Fund%20Manager%20Insights_as%20of%206.24.16_ ECM%20v2.pdf.

49. Eric Chaney and Laurence Boone, 'The die is caste [sic] – The future of the EU is in question', AXA, 24 June 2016, https://www.axa.com/en/ newsroom/news/brexit-the-future-of-the-eu-in-question-en.

50. Trefis Team, 'Can there be a silver lining for Diageo in the aftermath of the Brexit', *Forbes*, 27 June 2016, http://www.forbes.com/sites/greatspeculations/2016/06/27/can-there-be-a-silver-lining-for-diageo-in-the-aftermath-of-the-brexit/#719bdfba17c6. Jesse Riseborough, 'Rio Tinto commits to London head office after Brexit vote', *Bloomberg*, 3 July 2016, http://www.bloomberg.com/news/articles/2016-07-03/rio-tinto-chief-commits-to-london-head-office-after-brexit-vote-iq6nzyqq.

51. Edmund Shing, 'Brexit: Here are the three major winners from a weak pound right now', *International Business Times*, 6 July 2016, http://www.ibtimes.co.uk/brexit-fallout-rolls-royce-glaxosmithkline-experian-are-big-winners-weak-pound-1569154.

52. Ryan Dezember and Tim Puko, 'Meet two Brexit winners: BP and Royal Dutch Shell', *Wall Street Journal*, 24 June 2016, http://blogs.wsj.com/moneybeat/2016/06/24/meet-two-brexit-winners-bp-and-royal-dutch-shell/.

53. Will Martin, 'HSBC: Gold will explode if Britain votes for a Brexit', *Business Insider*, 15 June 2016, http://uk.businessinsider.com/eu-referendum-hsbc-note-on-brexit-and-the-price-of-gold-2016-6.

54. Rafi Farber, '2 stocks to buy post-Brexit', *24/7 Wall Street*, 16 June 2016, http://247wallst.com/investing/2016/06/16/2-stocks-to-buy-post-brexit/.

55. Jill Treanor, 'Ross McEwan on Brexit: it's not a banking crisis – RBS has plenty of money', *Guardian*, 17 July 2016, https://www.theguardian.com/business/2016/jul/17/ross-mcewan-rbs-brexit-not-banking-crisis-plenty-money and Lee Wild, 'Why Lloyds is a "buy" on Brexit blip', *Interactive Investor*, 13 June 2016, http://www.iii.co.uk/articles/325946/why-lloyds-buy-brexit-blip.

56. Ron Emler, 'Diageo shares surge after Brexit vote', *The Drinks Business*, 29 June 2016, https://www.thedrinksbusiness.com/2016/06/diageo-shares-surge-after-brexit-vote/. Matthew Campbell and Sam Chambers, 'A post-Brexit Britain offers silver linings for Diageo, BAT', *Bloomberg*, 27 June 2016, http://www.bloomberg.com/news/articles/2016-06-27/post-brexit-britain-offers-a-few-silver-linings-for-companies. Michael Scaturro, 'Vodafone revenues up despite decline

in UK sales', *Independent*, 22 July 2016,
http://www.independent.co.uk/news/business/news/vodafone-
results-revenues-up-despite-uk-sales-decline-a7149886.html.

57. BT, 'Brexit: the financial winners and losers following the vote', 5 July
2016, http://home.bt.com/lifestyle/money/mortgages-bills/brexit-
the-financial-winners-and-losers-following-the-vote-11364071832244.

Chapter 2

1. The Royal United Services Institute (RUSI) traces the decline of British
   military spending relative to France and Germany since WWII. The
   turning point came in 1990 with the origins of the first Gulf War. By
   the year 2000, Britain had joined America in bombing Iraq, invading
   Yugoslavia, and sending forces to East Timor and Sierra Leone.
   Another effect of increased military spending after 1990 was the
   elevation of British military power over that of France and Germany,
   making the trio the only European powers with a global reach. (Adrian
   L. Johnson (ed.), 2014, *Wars in Peace: British Military Operations since
   1991*, Royal United Services Institute, https://rusi.org/sites/default/
   files/wars_in_peace_foreword_and_intro.pdf.)

   On the 'exploitation' of resources, the British Ministry of Defence
   says: 'Globalisation is about the spread of capital, trade, intellectual
   property, economic activity, wealth and resources. It also encompasses
   the guaranteed access to and exploitation of these resources in developing states'. (MoD, 2010, *The Future Character of Conflict*, p. 43,
   https://www.gov.uk/government/uploads/system/uploads/
   attachment_data/file/486301/20151210-Archived_DCDC_
   FCOC.pdf.)

   On the so-called rules-based international system, Chatham House,
   for instance, says that Western liberal values are being undermined by
   sovereignty. This is not helped by the perception that somehow
   America does not abide by the 'rules' it preaches to others: 'the decision
   by the George W. Bush administration to invade Iraq in 2003 under a
   contested UN authorization continues to cast a long shadow over
   America's claim to be the principal defender of a rules-based international system. Questioning the legitimacy of US leadership has not

eased under Barack Obama, despite his more multilateral approach to problem-solving and reticence in using overt military force. The failure to close the Guantanamo Bay detention facility; the Senate report on the use of torture under the previous administration; the continued use of presidential authority under "war on terrorism" directives to carry out lethal drone strikes in the Middle East and Pakistan; and the exposure by Edward Snowden of the way US intelligence services used the dominance of US technology companies over the internet to carry out espionage – all have left the United States vulnerable to the accusation that it is as selective as any country about when it does and does not abide by the international norms and rules that it expects of others'. (Chatham House, 'Challenges to the Rules-Based International Order', 2015, Session 1, The London Conference, https://www.chathamhouse.org/sites/files/chathamhouse/ London%20Conference%202015%20-%20Background %20Papers.pdf.)

2. Vaughne Miller, 'Exiting the EU: impact in key UK policy areas', House of Commons Library, Briefing Paper, No. 07213, 12 February 2016, www.researchbriefings.files.parliament.uk/documents/CBP-7213/ CBP-7213.pdf and HMG, 2013, *Review of the Balance of Competences between the United Kingdom and the European Union: The Single Market*, https://www.gov.uk/government/uploads/system/uploads/ attachment_data/file/227069/2901084_SingleMarket_acc.pdf.

3. PwC, 'Attracting the BRICs: past trends and future prospects for inward investment into the UK', March 2013, http://www.pwc.co.uk/ services/economics-policy/insights/uk-economic-outlook/ ukeo-attracting-brics-march13.html.

4. HMG, op. cit.

5. For details and sources, see my *Britain's Secret Wars*, 2016, Clairview Books, pp. 1–15. On Nepal, see my 'Earthquake kills as many Nepalese as Britain's secret wars', Plymouth Institute for Peace Research, 28 April 2015, http://www.pipr.co.uk/all/earthquake-kills-as-many nepalese-as-britains-secret-war/. See also Thomas Bell, 2014, *Kathmandu*, Haus Publishing.

6. Secretary of State for Defence, 'Strategic Defence Review', July 1998,

http://archives.livreblancdefenseetsecurite.gouv.fr/2008/IMG/pdf/
sdr1998_complete.pdf.

7. HMG, 'National Security Strategy and Strategic Defence and Security
Review 2015: A Secure and Prosperous United Kingdom', Cm 9161,
November 2015, https://www.gov.uk/government/uploads/system/
uploads/attachment_data/file/478936/
52309_Cm_9161_NSS_SD_Review_PRINT_only.pdf.

8. Ibid.

9. Ibid.

10. Ibid. On Britain's colonial role in East Asia, see Christopher Bayly and
Tim Harper, 2008, *Forgotten Wars: The End of Britain's Asian Empire*,
Penguin. On Korea, see Thomas Hennessey, 2015, *Britain's Korean
War: Cold War diplomacy, strategy and security: 1950–53*, Manchester
University Press. On the background to Indonesia, see Matthew Jones,
1999, ' "Maximum disavowable aid": Britain, the United States and the
Indonesian rebellion, 1957–58', *The English Historical Review*, 114:
459, pp. 1179–1216. On the use of chemical weapons in Malaysia, see
Steven Rose, 'Chemical Weapons', *New Scientist*, 11 March 1982,
p. 630. For details of atrocities and archival sources, see Mark Curtis,
2003, *Web of Deceit*, Vintage, pp. 334–45.

11. HMG, 'National Security Strategy . . .', op. cit.

12. Ibid.

13. William Hague, 'Review of the Balance of Competences between the
United Kingdom and the European Union', July 2012,
https://www.gov.uk/government/uploads/system/uploads/
attachment_data/file/35431/eu-balance-of-competences-review.pdf.

14. Robert Hazell and Ben Young, 2012, *The Politics of Coalition: How the
Conservative-Liberal Democrat Government Works*, Hart Publishing.

15. David Cameron, 'Speech to Lord Mayor's Banquet', 15 November
2010, https://www.gov.uk/government/speeches/
speech-to-lord-mayors-banquet.

16. BBC News Online, 'David Cameron launches Indian trade drive', 28
July 2010, http://www.bbc.co.uk/news/mobile/uk-politics-
10784317. Foreign and Commonwealth Office, David Cameron and
Vince Cable, 'UK Prime Minister and Business Secretary welcome

£700 million Hawk', HMG, 28 July 2010, https://www.gov.uk/government/news/uk-prime-minister-and-business-secretary-welcome-700-million-hawk-deal. On nuclear-grade graphite exports to Israel, see for instance, Department for Business Innovation and Skills, 'Strategic Export Controls', Country Pivot Report, 1 January 2012 to 31 December 2012, p. 272.

17. One of the most serious outcomes of the Chilcot Inquiry into the invasion of Iraq was the admission by Foreign Secretary, Jack Straw, that the terrorist attacks on the Indian Parliament in December 2001 raised tensions to the point where 'a military engagement between India and Pakistan' was a 'probability'. Foreign Office spokesman John Williams said: the 'war might easily have gone nuclear'. While Straw tried to maintain the status quo, Britain continued exporting weapons to both sides, culminating with PM Blair's famous sale of Hawks to India in 2002. (PTI, 'UK feared India-Pakistan nuclear war in 2001: Iraq war inquiry', The Indian Express, 7 July 2016, http://indianexpress.com/article/india/india-news-india/iraq-war-inquiry-tony-blair-uk-india-pakistan-nuclear-war-2001-parliament-attack-2897918/.)

More recently, two prominent analysts reported that India and Pakistan were rehearsing separate nuclear war games. (Pervez Hoodbhoy and Zia Mian, 'Nuclear battles in South Asia', Bulletin of the Atomic Scientists, 4 May 2016, http://thebulletin.org/nuclear-battles-south-asia9415.)

On Lashkar-e-Toiba, see Mark Curtis, 2010, Secret Affairs, Serpent's Tail, pp. 218–87.

18. BBC News Online, 'David Cameron raises human rights in China talks', 9 November 2010, http://www.bbc.co.uk/news/business-11715216.

19. Laurence Martin and John Garnett, 1997, British Foreign Policy: Challenges and Choices for the 21st Century, Pinter, p. 38.

20. BBC, op. cit.

21. Raoul Ruparel, Stephen Booth and Vincenzo Scarpetta, 'Brexit guide: What next?', Open Europe, 2016, http://openeurope.org.uk/intelligence/britain-and-the-eu/guide-to-brexit/.

22. TTIP is the Transatlantic Trade and Investment Partnership. The European Commission says it will enable the EU to 'export more to the US and win government contracts; import more of the goods or services they need to make their final products; determine more easily when a product counts as being "Made in Europe" (or the USA); invest in the US more easily'. (EC, 'How TTIP would work', no date, http://ec.europa.eu/trade/policy/in-focus/ttip/about-ttip/contents/.) Cécile Barbière, 'France and Germany to form united front against ISDS', EurActiv, 15 January 2015, http://www.euractiv.com/section/trade-society/news/france-and-germany-to-form-united-front-against-isds/.

23. Ruperal et al., op. cit.

24. Lianna Brinded, 'I am starting to think a Brexit is a good idea, and I never thought I would ever say that', *Business Insider*, 15 June 2016, http://uk.businessinsider.com/eu-referendum-reasons-why-a-brexit-is-a-good-idea-2016-6 and Trades Union Congress, 'Workers contribute £32bn to UK economy from unpaid overtime', 27 February 2015, https://www.tuc.org.uk/economic-issues/labour-market/fair-pay-fortnight-2015/workplace-issues/workers-contribute-%C2%A332bn-uk.

Ajay Kapur, Niall Macleod and Narendra Singh, 'Plutonomy: Buying Luxury, Explaining Global Imbalances', Citigroup, Equity Strategy, Industry Note, 16 October 2005, p. 10.

25. Brinded, op. cit. and Brinded, 'This is why Britain should leave the EU if membership renegotiation fails', *Business Insider*, 23 June 2015, http://uk.businessinsider.com/eu-referendum-change-or-go-report-brexit-if-uk-renegotiation-of-eu-membership-fails-2015-6.

Reuters, 'British Chambers of Commerce says support growing for Brexit', 10 May 2016, http://uk.reuters.com/article/uk-britain-eu-bcc-idUKKCN0Y02LF.

26. Ruperal, op. cit.

27. Ibid. On the Tories' methods of crushing the Labour Party, consider the following: Part 3 of the Transparency of Lobbying, Non-party Campaigning and Trade Union Administration Act 2014 concerns trade unions and potentially allows the government, and by definition

private interests, access to trade union records. This, critics argue, will have a chilling effect on membership, which will lessen the amount of donations given by unions to the Labour Party.

Stephen Bush of the *New Statesman* writes that the Tories' constituency boundary changes will reduce the number of House of Commons seats from 650 to 600. Labour tends to have seats with fewer voters than their Tory counterparts. These variations will be 'eliminate[d]', says Bush, resulting in fewer seats for Labour. (Stephen Bush, 'Why are boundary changes bad for Labour?', *New Statesman* (The Staggers), 12 February 2016, http://www.newstatesman.com/politics/elections/2016/02/why-are-boundary-changes-bad-labour.)

28. Ruperal, op. cit.
29. HMG, op. cit.
30. Ibid.
31. Ted Bromund and Nile Gardiner, 'Freedom from the EU: Why Britain and U.S. Should Pursue a U.S.–U.K. Free Trade Area', Heritage Foundation, 26 September 2014, http://www.heritage.org/research/reports/2014/09/freedom-from-the-eu-why-britain-and-the-us-should-pursue-a-usuk-free-trade-area.
32. House of Commons Hansard, 'UK's Nuclear Deterrent', 18 July 2016, Volume 613, Column 568, https://hansard.parliament.uk/commons/2016-07-18/debates/16071818000001/UKSNuclearDeterrent.

    On the Falklands/Malvinas, see my 'Britain threatens nuclear attack on Argentina', Axis of Logic, 29 February 2012, http://axisoflogic.com/artman/publish/Article_64333.shtml.
33. Martin and Garnett, op. cit., p. 43. Raymond Lygo and Hugh Beach, 'On the security and military rationales for the UK retaining its nuclear weapons' in Ken Booth and Frank Barnaby (eds.), *The Future of Britain's Nuclear Weapons: Experts Reframe the Debate*, March 2006, Oxford Research Group and Beyond Trident, p. 29, http://www.oxfordresearchgroup.org.uk/sites/default/files/cdr28_0.pdf. MoD quoted in Hugh Beach, 'Tactical Nuclear Weapons: A British View', Pugwash, May 2014, https://pugwashconferences.files.wordpress.com/2014/05/20051210_london_rotblat_nw_beach.pdf.

34. Marshall Shepherd, 'How Theresa May's Geography Background Might Impact Her Leadership As UK's Next Prime Minister', *Forbes*, 12 July 2016, http://www.forbes.com/sites/marshallshepherd/2016/07/12/united-kingdoms-next-prime-minister-will-be-a-geographer-what-is-geography/#6059aa531f1c. Gov.uk, 'The Rt Hon Theresa May MP', no date, https://www.gov.uk/government/people/theresa-may. Aftab Ali, 'Home Office's "shocking treatment" of international students needs "urgent inquiry", says NUS', *Independent*, 11 April 2016, http://www.independent.co.uk/student/news/home-office-s-shocking-treatment-of-international-students-needs-urgent-inquiry-says-nus-a6979146.html.

35. Alex Morales, 'Hammond named UK Chancellor as economy suffers Brexit fallout', *Bloomberg*, 13 July 2016, http://www.bloomberg.com/news/articles/2016-07-13/hammond-named-u-k-chancellor-as-economy-suffers-brexit-fallout. For details and sources on Hammond's shocking role and statements, see my *Britain's Secret Wars*, 2016, Clairview Books, p. 205n12.

36. Boris Johnson, 'If Blair's so good at running the Congo, let him stay there', *Telegraph*, 10 January 2002, http://www.telegraph.co.uk/comment/personal-view/3571742/If-Blairs-so-good-at-running-the-Congo-let-him-stay-there.html. Johnson, 'The Boris archive: Africa is a mess, but we can't blame colonialism', *The Spectator*, 2 February 2002, http://blogs.spectator.co.uk/2016/07/boris-archive-africa-mess-cant-blame-colonialism/. Johnson, 'Getting our knickers in a twist over China', 1 September 2005, http://www.telegraph.co.uk/comment/personal-view/3619424/Getting-our-knickers-in-a-twist-over-China.html. RTÉ, 'Boris Johnson declares Wiff Waff is coming home', YouTube, 25 August 2008, https://www.youtube.com/watch?v=Uix9kXIMVRM. Douglas Murray, 'Boris Johnson wins *The Spectator*'s President Erdogan [sic] Offensive Poetry competition', *The Spectator*, 18 May 2016, http://blogs.spectator.co.uk/2016/05/boris-johnson-wins-the-spectators-president-erdogan-offensive-poetry-competition/. Alexandra Topping, 'Boris Johnson criticised for suggesting women go to university to find husband [sic]', *Guardian*, 8 July 2013, http://www.theguardian.com/politics/2013/jul/08/boris-

johnson-women-university-husband. Neil Tweedie, 'Boris in hot water over cannibalism in Papua', *Telegraph*, 9 September 2006, http://www.telegraph.co.uk/news/1528393/Boris-in-hot-water-over-cannibalism-in-Papua.html. Boris Johnson, 'Let's deal with the Devil: we should work with Vladimir Putin and Bashar al-Assad in Syria', *Telegraph*, 6 December 2015, http://www.telegraph.co.uk/news/worldnews/middleeast/syria/12036184/Lets-deal-with-the-Devil-we-should-work-with-Vladimir-Putin-and-Bashar-al-Assad-in-Syria.html. *Independent*, 'Boris Johnson "outed" journalist as an MI6 spy "for a laugh" ', *Independent*, 21 July, 2016, http://www.independent.co.uk/news/uk/politics/boris-johnson-outed-journalist-mi6-spy-laugh-foreign-secretary-dominic-lawson-a7148481.html.

37. On Britain and Idi Amin, see Mark Curtis, 2004, *Unpeople*, Vintage, pp. 245–62.

On Patel's career, see Operation Black Vote, 'Profile: Priti Patel', http://www.obv.org.uk/our-communities/profiles/obv-profile-priti-patel. Jamie Doward, 'Minister worked as spin doctor for tobacco giant that paid workers £15 a month', *Guardian*, 31 May 2015, https://www.theguardian.com/business/2015/may/30/priti-patel-worked-as-spin-doctor-tobacco-firm-burma-scandal. Truth Tobacco Industry Documents, https://www.industrydocumentslibrary.ucsf.edu/tobacco/docs/#id=nflf0205. Ian Silvera, 'Priti Patel: Who is the top Tory right-winger tipped to be the face of the Brexit campaign?', *International Business Times*, 8 February 2016, http://www.ibtimes.co.uk/priti-patel-who-top-tory-right-winger-tipped-be-face-brexit-campaign-1542619.

38. Kwasi Kwarteng, Priti Patel, Dominic Raab, Chris Skidmore and Elizabeth Truss, 2012, *Britannia Unchained: Global Lessons for Growth and Prosperity*, Palgrave Macmillan.

39. Liam Fox, 'Use of UK military forces in combat abroad', They Work For You, 'https://www.theyworkforyou.com/mp/10213/liam_fox/north_somerset/divisions?policy=6688

Fox told his Atlantic Bridge audience: 'For too many, peace has come to mean simply the absence of war. We cannot allow that corrosive view to go unchallenged'. (Jamie Doward, 'Liam Fox's Atlantic Bridge linked top Tories and Tea Party activists', *Guardian*, 15 October 2011, http://www.theguardian.com/politics/2011/oct/15/liam-fox-atlantic-bridge.)

Melissa Kite, 'Fox courts religious Right with plea to limit abortion to 12 weeks', *Telegraph*, 20 September 2005, http://www.telegraph.co.uk/news/uknews/3323922/Fox-courts-religious-Right-with-plea-to-limit-abortion-to-12-weeks.html.

40. Pink News, 'Liam Fox's "homophobic past" revealed', 9 March 2008, http://www.pinknews.co.uk/2008/03/09/liam-foxs-homophobic-past-revealed/. They Work For You, op. cit., https://www.theyworkforyou.com/mp/10213/liam_fox/north_somerset/divisions?policy=826. Ned Simons, 'Liam Fox Criticised for "Unethical" Decision to Open Trade Office in North Carolina', 27 July 2016, http://www.huffingtonpost.co.uk/entry/liam-fox-criticised-for-unethical-decision-to-open-trade-office-in-north-carolina_uk_57986b2fe4b0796a0b60cf4a. Nigel Nelson, 'Liam Fox expenses farce: Tory claims 3p for car journey of just 100 yards', *Mirror*, 5 October 2013, http://www.mirror.co.uk/news/uk-news/liam-fox-claims-3p-expenses-2342861. They Work For You, op. cit., https://www.theyworkforyou.com/mp/10213/liam_fox/north_somerset/divisions?policy=6670. Kim Sengupta, 'The tycoon and the conversation that did for Liam Fox', *Independent*, 17 October 2011, http://www.independent.co.uk/news/uk/politics/the-tycoon-and-the-conversation-that-did-for-liam-fox-2372012.html.

41. See my *Britain's Secret Wars*, 2016, Clairview Books, p. 99.

Chapter 3

1. David Graeber, 2013, *The Democracy Project: A History, a Crisis, a Movement*, Penguin.

The World Economic Forum, for instance, writes: 'there are around 420 regional trade agreements already in force around the world, according to the World Trade Organization ... [N]ot all are free trade agreements [sic]'. It quotes the Organization for Economic Cooperation and Development, which defines an FTA as 'countries within which tariffs and non-tariff trade barriers between the members are generally abolished but with no common trade policy toward non-members'. (Joe Myers, 'The world's free trade areas – and all you need to know about them', World Economic Forum, 6 May 2016, https://www.weforum.org/agenda/2016/05/world-free-trade-areas-everything-you-need-to-know/.)

2. John M. Culbertson describes free market ideology as 'a national theology', worshipped at the expense of domestic workers and living standards. He writes: 'Most American companies facing international competition have encountered the problem' of so-called *laissez-faire*. On distortions, Culbertson writes that '[m]ost governments are playing a simple game: they use their myriad powers – subsidies, favorable banking practices, local content requirements, exchange control and the like – to win jobs and gain higher incomes for their people or to achieve a favorable national balance of payments'. ('The Folly of Free Trade', *Harvard Business Review*, September 1986, https://hbr.org/1986/09/the-folly-of-free-trade.)

More recently, the US Chamber of Commerce wrote that American businesses continue to face higher tariffs than other countries. Nevertheless, FTAs have 'impressive benefits', says the report. In other words, barriers to trade (e.g., high tariffs) are overcome by distortions (e.g., subsidies). (US Chamber of Commerce, 'The Open Door of Trade: The Impressive Benefits of America's Free Trade Agreements', 2014, https://www.uschamber.com/sites/default/files/open_door_trade_report.pdf.)

3. Quoted in Miguel A. Maito and Eduardo Franciosi, 'A new incentive system for technological innovation in developing countries', World Health Organization, June 2011, http://www.who.int/phi/news/phi_12_fondo_innovador_MAM_EF_jun2011_en.pdf.

4. Global Justice Now, 'Leaked document shows Cameron sidelining UK parliament on controversial EU trade deal', 26 May 2016, http://www.globaljustice.org.uk/news/2016/may/26/leaked-document-shows-cameron-sidelining-uk-parliament-controversial-eu-trade-deal. Janyce McGregor, 'Life after Brexit', CBC News, 24 June 2016, http://www.cbc.ca/news/politics/brexit-ceta-canada-eu-trade-deal-1.3650708.

5. Matt Hancock of the Department for Business, Innovation and Skills, for instance, said in relation to foreign direct investment: since 2012, 'we've removed unnecessary burdens from business – around £1.5 billion per year has been saved by businesses as a result of our deregulation work'. ('Attracting foreign direct investment: UK government success', 23 September, 2014, https://www.gov.uk/government/speeches/attracting-foreign-direct-investment-uk-government-success.)

6. Brent Patterson of the left-wing grassroots organization, The Council of Canadians, points out that already, outside the CETA framework: 'if the Canada-European Union Comprehensive Economic and Trade Agreement (CETA) were ratified, it would pose a serious obstacle to the remunicipalization of privatized water services in England. That's because the Ontario Teachers' Pension Plan owns 27 per cent of Northumbrian Water Group Plc, which sells its water services to about 4.4 million 'customers' in England, and the Canada Pension Plan owns one-third of Anglian Water Services, which sells water services to approximately six million people in England'. (Patterson, 'CETA would lock-in water privatization in England', Council of Canadians, 14 January 2016, http://canadians.org/blog/ceta-would-lock-water-privatization-england.)

7. CETA, full text of the agreement, September 2014, European Commission, http://trade.ec.europa.eu/doclib/docs/2014/september/tradoc_152806.pdf.

8. Buffett said: 'There's class warfare, all right . . . but it's my class, the rich class, that's making war, and we're winning.' (Ben Stein, 'In class warfare, guess which class is winning', New York Times, 26 November 2006, http://www.nytimes.com/2006/11/26/business/yourmoney/26every.html?_r=0.) The Canadian Press, 'Brexit threatens "fine balance" of Canada-EU trade deal, Ed Fast says', CBC News, 8 July 2016, http://www.cbc.ca/news/politics/cp-ed-fast-canada-eu-trade-deal-brexit-1.3671069.

9. Joe Leahy, 'Brazil keen to open trade talks with UK', Financial Times, 22 July 2016, http://www.ft.com/cms/s/0/ce7cb3c0-4e9b-11e6-9b99-1e1f25294c08.html.

10. Gerson Freitas and Tatiana Freitas, 'As markets bemoan Brexit, Brazil beef shippers see opportunity', *Bloomberg*, 25 June 2016, http://www.bloomberg.com/news/articles/2016-06-24/as-markets-bemoan-brexit-brazil-beef-shippers-see-opportunity and Ruperal, op. cit.

11. William Blum, 2003, *Killing Hope*, Zed Books, pp. 163–72.

12. Emily Buchanan, 'How the UK taught Brazil's dictators interrogation techniques', BBC Magazine, 30 May 2014, http://www.bbc.co.uk/news/magazine-27625540 and BBC, 'Volkswagen "allowed torture" under Brazil military rule', 23 September 2015, http://www.bbc.co.uk/news/world-latin-america-34335094.

13. See, for example, Shihan Steve Costello, 'Shihan Steve's Acknowledgements of the Elite and Military Police', International Ryukyu Karate, 3 October 2011, http://www.ryukyukarate.info/news/shihan-steves-acknowledgements-of-the-elite-and-military-police. There is no suggestion that Costello or his business are involved in torture.

14. Katherine Trebeck, 'Is Brazil's social/economic miracle running out of steam just as the World Cup arrives?', Oxfam blogs, 4 June 2014, https://oxfamblogs.org/fp2p/is-brazils-socialeconomic-miracle-running-out-of-steam-just-as-the-world-cup-arrives/.

15. Mariana Ceratti and World Bank, 'How to Reduce Poverty: A New Lesson from Brazil for the World?', World Bank, 22 March 2014, http://www.worldbank.org/en/news/feature/2014/03/22/mundo-sin-pobreza-leccion-brasil-mundo-bolsa-familia and Francisco Vidal Luna and Herbert S. Klein, 2014, *The Economic and Social History of Brazil since 1889*, Cambridge University Press, p. 336.

16. Nacho Doce, 'Brazil's restive rich draft a duck to protest president', Reuters, 20 March 2016, http://www.reuters.com/article/us-brazil-politics-duck-idUSKCN0WM0F1.

17. Democracy Now!, 'This Confirms It was a Coup: Brazil Crisis Deepens as Evidence Mounts of Plot to Oust Dilma Rousseff', 25 May 2016, http://www.democracynow.org/2016/5/25/this_confirms_it_was_a_coup.

18. Brazilian Chamber of Commerce in GB, 'Brazil Business Brief', January 2016, 19:55, http://brazilianchamber.org.uk/sites/

brazilianchamber.org.uk/files/publications/BBB_Jan2016_
WEB_0.pdf

19. Costello, op. cit.

20. Tripp Mickle, 'Unrest in Brazil heightens concerns for marketers', *Sports Business*, 22 July 2013, http://www.sportsbusinessdaily.com/ Journal/Issues/2013/07/22/Marketing-and-Sponsorship/Brazil.aspx.

21. Amnesty USA, 'Surge in killings by policy sparks fear in favelas 100 days ahead of Rio Olympics', 26 April 2016, http://www.amnestyusa.org/news/press-releases/surge-in-killings-by-police-sparks-fear-in-favelas-100-days-ahead-of-rio-olympics.

22. Ibid. See also Department for Business, Innovation and Skills, 'Strategic Export Controls', Country Pivot Report, 1 Jan. 2012–31 Dec. 2012; The Stationery Office, pp. 80–88 and 2013 report, pp. 78–88.

23. The Channel Group, 'UK Trade Deal Tracker', 30 July 2016, http://thechannelgroup.org/insights/uk-trade-deal-tracker/.

24. Joseph Contreras, 2009, *In the Shadow of the Giant: The Americanization of Modern Mexico*, Rutgers University Press.

25. OECD, 'How's life in Mexico', live document, https://www.oecd.org.

26. Department for International Trade, 'Doing business in Mexico: Mexico trade and export guide', 10 May 2016, https://www.gov.uk/ government/publications/exporting-to-mexico/exporting-to-mexico.

27. Ibid.

28. Ibid.

29. On labour market 'flexibility', see Allister Heath, 'Labour market flexibility has saved the UK – so don't bash it', City AM, 1 May 2014, http://www.cityam.com/article/1398915632/labour-market-flexibility-has-saved-uk-so-don-t-bash-it.

On OECD standards, see OECD, 'In it together: Why less inequality benefits all … in the United Kingdom', 21 May 2015, http://www.oecd.org/unitedkingdom/OECD2015-In-It Together-Highlights-UnitedKingdom-Embargo-21May11amPArisTime.pdf. Worker-participation.eu, 'Trade Unions', no date, http://www.worker-participation.eu/National-Industrial-Relations/Countries/United-Kingdom/Trade-Unions. OECD, 'Trade Union Density', no date, https://stats.oecd.org/Index.aspx?DataSetCode=UN_DEN.

30. AFL-CIO, 'Mexico: Labor Rights Concerns', no date, http://www.aflcio.org/Issues/Trade/Trans-Pacific-Partnership-Free-Trade-Agreement-TPP/Labor-Rights/Mexico-Labor-Rights-Concerns.

31. Amnesty International, 'Mexico: Sexual violence routinely used as torture to secure "confessions" from women', 28 June 2016, https://www.amnesty.org/en/latest/news/2016/06/mexico-sexual-violence-routinely-used-as-torture-to-secure-confessions-from-women/.

32. Human Rights Watch, 'Mexico's Disappeared', 20 February 2013, https://www.hrw.org/report/2013/02/20/mexicos-disappeared/enduring-cost-crisis-ignored.

33. Sara Mojtehedzadeh, 'Extortion, threats, kidnapping: Workers the hidden casualty of Mexico's violence', *Toronto Star*, 23 May 2016, https://www.thestar.com/news/gta/2016/05/23/extortion-threats-kidnapping-workers-the-hidden-casualty-of-mexicos-violence.html.

34. Department for Business, Innovation and Skills, 'Strategic Export Controls', Country Pivot Report: 1st January 2014–31st December 2014, The Stationery Office.

35. Elite UK Forces, 'SAS capture IS commanders', 9 May 2016, http://www.eliteukforces.info/uk-military-news/09052016-sas-head-hunting.php. Elite UK Forces, 'British Special Forces in Syria frontline role', 7 June 2016, http://www.eliteukforces.info/uk-military-news/07062016-british-special-forces-syria.php. Elite UK Forces, 'Libya: British Special Forces take out ISIS truck with missile', 26 May 2016, http://www.eliteukforces.info/uk-military-news/26052016-sas-blow-up-trucks-libya.php. David Gardner, 'Captured with $2 million in cash, the drugs baron who stewed enemies in boiling oil and beheaded hundreds', *Daily Mail*, 16 July 2013, http://www.dailymail.co.uk/news/article-2364911/Captured-2million-cash-drugs-baron-stewed-enemies-boiling-oil-beheaded-hundreds.html. LiveLeak, '3 men skinned alive and beheaded by a drug cartel', 16 March 2013, http://www.liveleak.com/browse?q=zeta%20cartel&sort_by=comments.

36. Natasha Bertrand, 'How 34 commandos created Mexico's most brutal drug cartel', *Business Insider*, 5 March 2015, http://uk.businessinsider.com/how-34-commandos-created-mexicos-most-brutal-drug-cartel-2015-3?r=US&IR=T.

37. Cartel Chronicles, 'Mexican cartel and politicians' money laundering network exposed and unraveling', Breitbart, 27 November 2015, http://www.breitbart.com/texas/2015/11/27/los-zetas-money-laundering-network-continues-unravel/.

38. Fox News Latino, 'Mexican Mayor Maria Santos Gorrostieta Killed by Gunmen was Defiant to the End', 28 November 2012, http://latino.foxnews.com/latino/news/2012/11/28/mexican-mayor-maria-santos-gorrostieta-killed-by-gunmen-was-defiant-to-end/ and Reuters, 'Mayoral candidate Aide Nava decapitated in Mexico's Guerrero state', 3 November 2015, http://www.huffingtonpost.com/2015/03/11/aide-nava-decapitated_n_6849232.html.

39. OEC, 'United States', MIT, http://atlas.media.mit.edu/en/profile/country/usa/.

40. Neil Gardiner, 'A US-UK free trade agreement would be good for Britain and America', CAPX, 9 March 2015, http://capx.co/a-us-uk-free-trade-agreement-would-be-good-for-britain-and-america/.

41. Daniel Hannan, 'Free Britain to trade with the world', Financial Times, 21 June 2016, http://www.ft.com/cms/s/2/6d4a444a-36f5-11e6-a780-b48ed7b6126f.html. Gardiner and Bromund, op. cit. Giles Scott-Smith, 2008, Networks of Empire: The US State Department's Foreign Leader Program in the Netherlands, France, and Britain 1950–1970, Peter Lang. See also Scott-Smith's 'Searching for the successor generation: Public diplomacy, the US Embassy's International Visitor Program and the Labour Party in the 1980s', British Journal of Political and International Relations, Vol. 8., 2006, pp. 214–37. Robin Ramsay, 2008, Politics and Paranoia, Picnic, p. 219.

42. On issues of nationalization and the opinion of Tory voters, see Preface, endnote 2.

43. For a scholarly account of the Skull and Bones, see Alexandra Robbins, 2002, Secrets of the Tomb: Skull and Bones, the Ivy League, and the Hidden Paths of Power, Little, Brown. For a more dissident perspective, citing leaked materials, see Antony C. Sutton, 2002, America's Secret Establishment: An Introduction to the Order of Skull and Bones, Trine Day. Margaret Thatcher, 2003, Statecraft: Strategies for a Changing World, Harper Perennial.

44. Gardiner and Bromund, op. cit.

45. Ibid.

46. Ibid. Corporate Europe Observatory, 'Agribusiness is the biggest lobbyist on the EU–US trade deal, new research reveals', 8 July 2014, http://corporateeurope.org/pressreleases/2014/07/agribusiness-biggest-lobbyist-eu-us-trade-deal-new-research-reveals.

Chapter 4

1. Lawrence Talbot (Dana Gould) (writer), 'Goo Goo Gai Pan', *The Simpsons*, Season 16, Episode 12, Fox.

2. IMF, 'Gross domestic product based on purchasing-power-parity (PPP) per capita GDP', 2015, http://www.imf.org.
   United Nations Development Programme, 'Table 1: Human Development Index and its components', 2014 data, http://hdr.undp.org/en/composite/HDI. World Health Organization, 'Water Sanitation', 2012, http://www.who.int/water_sanitation_health/monitoring/jmp2012/fast_facts/en/.

3. OEC, 'China (CHN) Exports, Imports, and Trade Partners', 2014, atlas.media.mit.edu/en/profile/country/.

4. Jan Drahokoupil, Rutvica Andrijasevic and Devi Sacchetto (eds), 'Flexible workforces and low profit margins: electronics assembly between Europe and China', European Trades Union Institute, 2016, ETUI.

5. International Labor Organization and World Bank, 'Labor force, total', 2014 data, http://data.worldbank.org/indicator/SL.TLF.TOTL.IN.

6. AFL-CIO, 'Labor Rights in China', no date, http://www.aflcio.org/Issues/Trade/China/Labor-Rights-in-China. Amnesty International, 'China: No end in sight — torture and forced confessions in China', 12 November 2015, https://www.amnesty.org/en/documents/asa17/2731/2015/en/.

7. Foreign and Commonwealth Office, 'UK–China Joint Statement 2015', 22 October 2015, https://www.gov.uk/government/news/uk-china-joint-statement-2015. College of Policing, 'The Strategic Command Course 2016', 2015, http://www.college.police.uk/What-we-do/

Learning/Curriculum/Leadership/Documents/SCC_-_info_for_
international_non_HO_and_partners.pdf.

8. HM Treasury and George Osborne, 'China chooses London for its first
ever sovereign renminbi (RMB) bond issued outside of China',
Government website, 26 May 2016, https://www.gov.uk/government/
news/china-chooses-london-for-its-first-ever-sovereign-renminbi-rmb-
bond-issued-outside-of-china.

9. Ibid.

10. Ibid.

11. Phillip Inman, Terry Macalister, Gwyn Topham and Mark Sweney,
'The UK's deals worth billions with China: what do they really mean?',
Guardian, 24 October 2015, https://www.theguardian.com/business/
2015/oct/24/britains-deals-with-china-billions-what-do-they-mean.

12. Treasury and Osborne, op. cit.

13. Kamal Ahmed, 'UK explores multi-billion pound free trade deal with
China', 24 July 2016, BBC News Online,
http://www.bbc.co.uk/news/business-36877573.

14. University of Sheffield and Sheffield Chamber of Commerce, 'Sheffield
prepares for new era of UK–China trade', 26 July 2016,
https://www.sheffield.ac.uk/news/nr/sheffield-china-trade-gateway-
1.593506.

15. Vijayashree Mathad and S. Shivprasad, 'Malnutrition: A Daunting
Problem for India's Spectacular Growth', *Indian Journal of Clinical
Practice*, 23:11, April 2013, pp. 760–64. World Bank, 'Mortality rate,
infant (per 1,000 live births)', no date,
http://data.worldbank.org/indicator/SP.DYN.IMRT.IN. UN, 'Table 1:
Human Development Index',
http://hdr.undp.org/en/composite/HDI.

16. OEC, 'India', MIT, http://atlas.media.mit.edu/en/visualize/tree_map/
hs92/export/ind/all/show/2014/.

17. Ibid. Rumani Saikia Phukan, 'Child Labour in Diamond Industry
Continues in India Despite Abolition', *Maps of India*, 8 February 2015,
http://www.mapsofindia.com/my-india/government/child-labour-in-
diamond-industry-in-india-it-will-continue-why. (The report points out
that 90% of the world's diamonds are cut in India and that companies

prefer child labourers because of their eyesight and dexterity.) SOMO (Centre for Research on Multinational Corporations) and ICN (India Committee of the Netherlands), 'Flawed Fabrics: The abuse of girls and women workers in the South Indian textile industry', October 2014, http://www.indianet.nl/pdf/FlawedFabrics.pdf. Devin Finn, 'Bonded Labor in India', *Tropical Research Digest*, http://www.du.edu/korbel/hrhw/researchdigest/slavery/india.pdf.

18. Gregory Shaffer, James Nedumpara and Aseema Sinha, 'State transformation and the role of lawyers: The WTO, India and transnational legal ordering', *Law and Society Review*, 49:3, 2015, pp. 595–629. See also Jean Drèze and Amartya Sen, 1987, *Hunger and Public Action*, Claredon Press, pp. 204–225.

19. En. I. Bālaṛām, 1967, *A short history of the Communist Party of India*, Prabhat Book House. Rabindra Ray, 1992, *The Naxalites and their ideology*, Oxford University Press. Ross Mallick, 1994, *India communism: Opposition, collaboration, and institutionalization*, Oxford University Press. Neil Redfern, 2005, *Class or Nation: Communists, Imperialism, and Two World Wars*, Tauris Academic Studies. Sudeep Chakravarti, 2008, *Red Sun: Travels in Naxalite Country*, Penguin. D.N. Gupta, 2008, *Communism and Nationalism in Colonial India, 1939–45*, SAGE.

20. Shaffer et al., op. cit.

21. Ibid.

22. Partha Sarathi Ghosh, 1999, *BJP and the Evolution of Hindu Nationalism: From Periphery to Centre*, Manohar Publishers. Centre for Indian Political Research and Analysis, 2002, *Fascism on Rise: The Emergence of Hindu Reactionary Right*, Christophe Jaffrelot, 2009, *Hindu Nationalism: A Reader*, Princeton University Press.

23. Arundhati Roy, 2014, *Capitalism: A Ghost Story*, Verso. MoD, 'Indian troops complete joint training exercise on Salisbury Plain', 23 August 2011, https://www.gov.uk/government/news/indian-troops-complete-joint-training-exercise-on-salisbury-plain.

24. Business, Innovation and Skills, op. cit.

25. Simon Mundy and Amy Kazmin, 'India accentuates the positive on Brexit', *Financial Times*, 27 June 2016, http://www.ft.com/cms/s/0/d35362a0-3c57-11e6-8716-a4a71e8140b0.html.

26. Ibid.
27. Department for International Trade, 'Doing business in India: India trade and export guide', 17 February 2016, https://www.gov.uk/government/publications/exporting-to-india/exporting-to-india.
28. Ibid.
29. United Nations Development Programme, 'Table 1: Human Development Index and its components', 2014 data, http://hdr.undp.org/en/composite/HDI. MIT, 'South Korea', 2014, http://atlas.media.mit.edu/en/profile/country/kor/. OECD, 'Korea', no date, http://www.oecd.org/korea/.
30. M. Hart-Landsberg and P. Burkett, 'Economic crisis and restructuring in South Korea: beyond the free market-statist debate', *Critical Studies*, 2001, 33:3, pp. 403–30.
31. Kwan S. Kim, 'The Korean Miracle (1962-1980) Revisited: Myths and Realities in Strategy and Development', Working Paper 166, November 1991, Kellogg Institute, https://kellogg.nd.edu/publications/workingpapers/WPS/166.pdf.
32. Ibid.
33. Ibid.
34. Ibid.
35. European Commission, 'Countries and regions: South Korea', 2016, http://ec.europa.eu/trade/policy/countries-and-regions/countries/south-korea/index_en.htm.
36. *Wall Street Journal*, 'South Korea's Brexit Example', 26 June 2016, http://www.wsj.com/articles/south-koreas-brexit-example-1466960252.
37. Nick Lyne, 'A renewed focus on cooperation', *First*, pp. 28–29, www.firstmagazine.com/DownloadSpecialReportDetail.1484.ashx.
38. Ibid.
39. WSJ, op. cit.

Conclusion

1. Nigel Lawson, 'Brexit gives us a chance to finish the Thatcher revolution', *Financial Times*, 2 September 2016, https://www.ft.com/content/6cb84f70-6b7c-11e6-a0b1-d87a9fea034f.

2. Nigel Lawson, 1992, *The View from Number 11: Memoirs of a Tory Radical*, Bantam.

3. Lawson, 'Brexit gives us...', op. cit.

4. Lord Ashcroft Polls, 'How the United Kingdom voted on Thursday ... and why', 24 June 2016, http://lordashcroftpolls.com/2016/06/how-the-united-kingdom-voted-and-why/.

5. Kylie MacLellan and Sarah Young, 'UK announces rapid strike forces, more warships in new defence plan', Reuters, 23 November 2015, http://uk.reuters.com/article/uk-britain-defence-idUKKBN0TC0V120151123.

6. The documents can be acquired via Greenpeace UK, 'Exposed: Canada's secret tar sands lobbying of UK ministers', 27 November 2011, http://www.greenpeace.org.uk/blog/climate/exposed-canadas-secret-tar-sands-lobbying-uk-ministers-20111127.

7. Ibid. and Donald Macintyre, 'Government accused of launching "attack on local democracy" with new council investment rule', *Independent*, 26 December 2015, http://www.independent.co.uk/news/uk/politics/government-accused-of-launching-attack-on-local-democracy-with-new-council-investment-rule-a6786916.html.

8. Go Fossil Free, 'How much does your council invest in fossil fuels?', http://gofossilfree.org/uk/pensions/.

9. Foreign and Commonwealth Office and James David Bevan, 'The UK and India: four myths and a big idea', 29 September 2012, https://www.gov.uk/government/speeches/the-uk-and-india-four-myths-and-a-big-idea and Vicki Owen, 'Big leap in small UK companies farming out jobs to workers overseas', *This is Money*, 2 August 2014, http://www.thisismoney.co.uk/money/smallbusiness/article-2714300/Big-leap-small-UK-companies-farming-jobs-workers-overseas.html.

10. The BBC's Mark Mardell asks, amusingly: 'What does "Brexit means Brexit" mean?', 14 July 2016, http://www.bbc.co.uk/news/uk-politics-36782922.

Parliamentary Secretary, John Penrose, says: 'The question of how to invoke parliamentary discussion around triggering article 50 [sic] has two distinct facets, one legal and the other democratic. Taking the legal considerations first, I am sure that everyone will be aware of the debate about whether invoking article 50 can be done through the royal prerogative, which would not legally require parliamentary approval, or would require an Act of Parliament because it leads ultimately to repeal or amendment of the European Communities Act 1972 … Government lawyers believe that it is a royal prerogative issue'. (Hansard, 'Article 50: Parliamentary Approval', 11 July Column 23, https://hansard.parliament.uk/commons/2016-07-11/debates/ 1607114000002/Article50ParliamentaryApproval.)

11. On the merging of investment banks and commercial banks, Lawson said: 'I didn't give it a great deal of thought … But it was a completely unforeseen consequence' of the Big Bang. (BBC Radio 4, 'Glass-Steagall: A Price Worth Paying?', 1 February, 2010, http://www.bbc.co.uk/radio/player/b00qbxwj.)

Index